COMMUNICATION AND EDUCATIONAL TECHNOLOGY

FOR B.SC.NURSING STUDENTS AS PER INC SYLLABUS

MONIKA DEVI NR

I dedicated this work to my mother who always consecrates me that "always faith in God" and "he will always be with us". And to my family for constant support and faith in me, and my beloved husband for encouraging and motivating me in my work

Contents

PREFACE

It gives me immense gratification to write the preface of the "Textbook of communication and Educational Technology" I hope this book found to be quite helpful for the nursing students in their venture.

This book is written for graduate nursing students to meet the need of their study requirements about communication and Educational Technology in nursing.

I hope this book will be very helpful for not only students of nursing and as well as the teaching faculty also. If Any suggestions for further improvement in the text will be highly appreciated and thankfully acknowledged by the writers as well as the publisher.

It is my hope that the content, style, and organizations of this book continue to meet the need of students.

Your productive criticisms and precious suggestions for improvements are welcome.

With all warm wishes to the readers.

Monika Devi NR

Acknowledgements

ACKNOWLEDGMENTS
First and foremost I would like to thank almighty God for His grace and blessings, and also for giving me courage and paving my path for the work without much difficulty.
I am extremely thankful to my teacher Dr. Kamli Prakash, for her guidance and encouragement.
My immense love and gratitude to my loving Mother Mrs. Sita Devi, beloved brother Mr. Ajay Kumar, Sister in law Deepika and I am deeply gratified to my beloved husband Mr. Anil Kumar, Sister Mrs. Geeta Devi, brother in law Mr. Pawan Kumar, and my younger sister Ms. Deepika for their constant support, encouragement and love towards me and for always motivating me for my work.
I want to pay my sincere thanks to all the Staff of Notion Publisherfor giving me the opportunity and their cooperation and support during the process of publication.
With Thankful Heart

Monika Devi NR

<h1 style="text-align:center">I</h1>

Review of communication process

Introduction of Communications

The term communication has been derived from the Latin word, 'communis', which means common. Communication means, to tell, show, spread information, and inform. The term communication is used to signify the process of transferring ideas or receiving them by any means such as word of mouth, telephone, telegram, letter, message, etc. Thus, communication stands for sharing of information, imparting or conveying ideas and knowledge.

Meaning

The English word 'communication' is derived from the Latin word communis, which means common. The term communication refers to the sharing of ideas in common. In other words, it is the transmission and interaction of facts, ideas, opinions, feelings, or attitudes. Communication is the essence of management. The basic function of management (planning, organizing, staffing, directing, and controlling) cannot be performed well without effective communication.

In short, Communication is the process of passing ideas, views, facts, information, and understanding from one person to another. This process is necessary for making the subordinates understand what the management expects from them.

Communication cannot take place without two parties – the receiver and the sender. The information which is sent by the sender must be understandable to the receiver.

Definition:

Following are some of the important definitions of communication: Communication may be defined as "the transfer of information and understanding from oneØ person to another."

According to Koontz and O'Donnel, Communication may be understood "as the exchange of information at least between two persons to create an understanding in the mind of the other, whether or not it gives rise to conflict."

Newman and Summer- "Communication is an exchange of facts, ideas, opinions or emotions by two or more persons."

'Communication is the sum of all things a person does when he wants to create an understanding in the mind of another. – Louis A. Allen

'It is the process of passing information and understanding from one person to another. It is essentially a bridge of meaning between people. By using this bridge of meaning, a person can safely cross the river of misunderstanding that separates all the people'. – Keith Davis.

Purposes of communications

The primary objective of communication in management is to convey information—instructions, policies, procedures, decisions, etc., so the listener will hear, read, understand what is said, agree and accept the message, and react as intended by the manager or sender of the communication. There are many objectives of communication. They are

- Stronger Decision Making

- Increased Productivity
- Steadier Workflow
- Enhanced Professional Image
- Clearer Promotional Material
- Provide Advice
- Provide Order
- Suggestion
- Persuasion
- Education
- Warning
- Raising Morale
- & Motivation To Give
- & Receive information To Provide Counseling
- To Improve Discipline

Characteristics of Communication

The characteristics of communication are as follows:

i. **At least two persons** – Communication involves at least two persons—the sender and the receiver. The sender sends the message and the receiver receives the message. There is an exchange of information between two or more persons.

ii. **Two-way process** – Communication is essentially a two-way process. It does not merely mean sending and receiving messages. It is not complete unless and until the message has been understood by the receiver in the same sense.

iii. **Form of communication** – Communication may take several forms, e.g., order, instruction, report, queries, etc. It may be verbal or written. It may be formal or informal.

iv. **Scope** – Communication is present in all human relationships. It is essential in all types of organizations and at all levels of management. It has a very wide scope.

v. **Dynamic process** – Communication is influenced by the mood and thinking of the sender and receiver. It keeps on changing depending upon the Level of understanding of the sender and receiver.

vi. **Goal-oriented** – Communication is goal-oriented and is effective only when there is a congruence of goals of the sender and the receiver.

vii. **Interdisciplinary** – Communication derives knowledge from several sciences like anthropology (the study of body language), sociology (the study of human behavior), psychology (the study of a human), etc. The linking between these sciences makes communication effective.

viii. **Interpersonal relations** – The main purpose of communication is to influence the human behavior which creates interpersonal relations.

ix. **Circular process** – There is a circular flow of information in the communication process. After the feedback, the receiver of the original message is required to transmit another message. The response indicates the success of the communication.

Elements of Communication Process:

The communication is a dynamic process that begins with the conceptualizing of ideas by the sender who then transmits the message through a channel to the receiver, who in turn gives the feedback in the form of some message or signal within the given time frame. Thus, there are Seven major elements of communication process:

1. Sender: The sender or the communicator is the person who initiates the conversation and has conceptualized the idea that he intends to convey it to others.

2. Encoding: The sender begins with the encoding process wherein he uses certain words or non-verbal methods such as symbols, signs, body gestures, etc. to translate the information into a message. The sender's knowledge, skills, perception, background, competencies, etc. has a great impact on the success of the message.

3. Message: Once the encoding is finished, the sender gets the message that he intends to convey. The message can be written, oral, symbolic or non-verbal such as body gestures, silence, sigh's, sounds, etc. or any other signal that triggers the response of a receiver.

4. Communication Channel: The Sender chooses the medium through which he wants to convey his message to the recipient. It must be selected carefully in order to make the message effective and correctly interpreted by the recipient. The choice of medium depends on the interpersonal relationships between the sender and the receiver and also on the urgency of the message being sent. Oral, virtual, written, sound, gesture, etc. are some of the commonly used communication mediums.

5. Receiver: The receiver is the person for whom the message is intended or targeted. The communication process has the following components:

- **Sender or communicator** – Sender is an employee with ideas, intentions, information, and a purpose for communicating. He is the source or initiator of the communication. He has something with a meaning to communicate. Communication begins when a sender identifies the need to send a message based on certain reasons.
- **Message** – The sender encodes meaning into a message that can be transmitted. The message represents the meaning, the source is trying to convey.
- **Encoding** – The function of encoding is to provide a form in which ideas and purpose can be expressed as a message. The result of the encoding process is the message. Encoding involves translating the sender's intent or ideas into a systematic set of symbols or gestures.
- **Channel or medium** – A medium serves as the means of communication whereas a channel refers to the means of transmission of a message between the sender and the receiver. A medium, which is an abstraction, can be oral, written, or non-verbal. Channel, on the other hand, is concrete and could be a letter, a report, a book, a memorandum, fax, an email, the television, the telephone, etc. A sender conveys his/her message to the receiver by some medium (oral, written, or nonverbal) over some channel (electronic means or printed Media).
- **Receiver** – The receiver is the individual whose senses perceive the sender's message. There may be one or many receivers. If the message does not reach the receiver, communication is not completed.
- **Decoding** – Decoding is the process by which the receiver interprets the message and translates it into meaningful information. Decoding is a two-step process – (a) the receiver must first perceive the message, and (b) the receiver must then interpret it. The decoding process is very much affected by some factors such as the receiver's need, status, experience, situational factors, etc.
- **Communication noise** – In communication, noise can be thought of as those factors that disturb or distort the intended message. Noise may occur in each of the elements of communication. "Noise" hinders communication. It includes the following factors:

  - Factors that hinder the development of clear thought.
  - Faulty encoding due to ambiguous symbols.
  - Defects in the channel.
  - Inattentive reception.
  - Faulty decoding due to prejudices, wrong under-standing, personal outlook, the wrong meaning of words and symbols. Noise can result in miscommunication. Hence the important point is to realize all these possibilities of noise and to minimize them.

- **Feedback** – A feedback provides a link or channel for the communicator to know the receiver's response and to determine whether the message has been received and has produced the intended change. Feedback may come in many ways. In face-to-face communication, feedback comes through the facial expressions of the receiver. Some indirect means of feedback are such factors as declines in productivity, poor quality of production, lack of coordination, absenteeism, etc. Feedback may cause the sender to modify his future communication.

Types of communication:

There are several types of communication in our practical life. It depends on an organizational pattern; parties of organization involved; several workers, the pattern of activating, etc. the types of communication are shown below in a diagram:

A. Based on parties

1. External communication: External communication is the process of exchanging information with the people of various external or outside parties of the organization. Generally, these parties are a stakeholder of the organization.

2. Internal communication: Internal communication is the process of exchanging information among people of different levels or internal participants within the organization.

- Horizontal communication: Horizontal communication is the communication where information or messages flows between or among the parallel or same level or statuses people of the organizational structure.
- Vertical communication: Vertical communication is the communication where information or messages flows between or among the subordinates and superiors of the organization.
- Downward communication: Downward communication is the communication where information or messages flows from the top of the organizational structure from the bottom of the organizational structure.
- Upward communication: Upward communication is the communication where information or messages flows from the down/bottom of the organizational structure to the top of the organizational structure.
- Cross or diagonal communication: Diagonal or cross-communication occurs when information flows between persons at different levels who have no direct reporting relationship. It is used to speed information flow, to improve understanding to coordination etc. for the achievement of the organization.

B. Based on formality
Formal communication:

- Formal communication is the process of exchanging information by following the prescribed or official rules, procedures, systems formalities, chain of command etc. in the organizational structure.
- Informal communiceation: Informal communication is the process of spontaneous exchange of information among various people of different status in the organizational structure.

C. Based on media

- Written communication: Written communication is the process of communication in which messages or information is exchanged or communicated within sender and receiver through written form.
- Oral or verbal communication: Oral or verbal communication is the process of communication in which messages or information is exchanged or communicated within sender and receiver through using any spoken or written word.
- Non-verbal communication: Non-verbal communication is the process of communication in which messages or information is exchanged or communicated within sender and receiver through without using any spoken or written word.

D. Others Mass communication:

Mass communication is a process of transmitting information, thoughts, opinions or attitude through specific channel or media to a large number of heterogeneous audiences.

- Personal communication: When people exchanged information related to their personal life or personal affair is known as personal communication.
- Interpersonal communication: Interpersonal communication occurs when two individuals are involved or exchanging information, ideas, opinions, feelings relating to the personal, social, organizational, national and international matter who are located in the same place. It is a process of face-to-face communication between individuals where messages may be verbal (that is, expressed in words) or they may not involve words at all but consist of gestures, facial expressions, and certain postures (body language).

1. Verbal Communication: The communication happens through verbally, vocally or through written words which express or convey the message to other is called verbal communication. Example: Baby crying (vocal) is verbal communication which express the hungry or pain through vocally. Verbal communication has classified into two types: A . Oral Communication

B. Written Communication. Apart from oral and written, verbal communication is also has following types:

- Public Communication,
- Small Group Communication
- Intrapersonal Communication
- Interpersonal Communication

Types of Verbal Communication:

A. Oral Communication: A communication which happens through word of mouth, spoken Words, conversations and also any messages or information are shared or exchanged between one another through speech or word of mouth is called oral communication. Example: Public speech, News reading, Television, Radio, telephone and mobile conversations.

B. Written Communication: A communication happens through any word written or often written sign which refers the languages uses in any medium is called written communication. Example: Simply any hand written, typed, Newspaper, printed word documents, letters, books and magazines. There are also other four types of verbal communication, which are listed below:

A. Public Communication: The public communication is defined as the communication of a person with the public. It involves a massive assembly of people. For example, the Prime Minister addressing the public about the multiple developing projects; Other examples include elections, campaigns, public speeches, etc.

B. Small-Group Communication: The small group communication is defined as communication within two or more people. The number of people participating in such communication is enough to have a good interaction with each other; For example, school meetings, board meetings, press conferences, office meetings, team meetings, family gatherings, etc.

C. Intrapersonal Communication: Intrapersonal communication is communication within us. It is also called as internal communication. It includes self-thinking, analysis, thoughts, assessments, etc. associated with the inner state of mind. The person's internal thoughts or feelings play a vital role in intrapersonal communication. It also includes various activities, such as solo speaking, solo writing, solo dancing, concentration, and self-awareness.

D. Interpersonal Communication: Interpersonal communication is the communication between us and others over the channel.

The communication can be online, face-to-face, video conference on mobile, etc. Interpersonal skills are essential, whether we are a manager, employee, or looking for work. Such skills are also known as soft skills that determine how well a person can communicate, behave, and relate to others.

2. Non-Verbal Communication:

Any communication without word of mouth, spoken words, Conversation and written languages are called Non-Verbal Communication. It happens through Signs, symbols, colors, gestures, body language or any facial expressions are known as non-verbal communication. Examples: Traffic signals are one of the best examples for non-verbal communication.

Types of Non-verbal Communication

1. Kinesics Body Movements Gestures and Body Stance Facial Expressions Eyes Movements
2. Proxemics
3. Haptics
4. Chronemics
5. Paralanguage
6. Appearance
7. Artifacts
8. Environment

1. KINESICS: a. Body language is a type of a nonverbal communication in which physical behaviors are used to express or convey the information. Such behavior includes facial expressions, body posture, gestures, eye movement, touch and the use of space. Interpretations of human body language. It is also known as kinesics.

b. Facial expression is a part of body language and the expression of emotions such as the movement of the eyes, eyebrows, lips, nose and cheeks. The face displays numerous emotions such as: Happiness, Surprise, Disgust, Anger, Sadness, etc...

c. Head and neck signals: The body language of the head should be considered in conjunction with that of the neck. Body language conveyed by the head and neck involves various ranges of movement. Nodding of the head is generally considered as a sign of saying 'yes'. Shaking the head is usually interpreted as meaning 'no'.

d. Body postures: Emotions can also be detected through body postures. For example, a person feeling angry would portray dominance over the other, and their posture would display approach tendencies. Sitting or standing postures also indicate one's emotions. A person sitting till the back of their chair, leans forward with their head nodding along with the discussion implies that they are open, relaxed and generally ready to listen. On the other hand, a person who has their legs and arms crossed with the foot kicking slightly implies that they are feeling impatient and emotionally detached from the discussion

e. Gestures - Gestures are movements made with body parts (example hands, arms, fingers, head, legs) and they may be voluntary or involuntary. Different hand gestures help emphasize meanings and regulate interaction between or among participants. For Example: Relaxed hands indicate confidence and self-assurance, while clenched hands may be interpreted as signs of stress or anger. If a person is wringing their hands, this demonstrates nervousness and anxiety.

f. Oculesics - Oculesics, a subcategory of body language, is the study of eye movement, eye behavior, gaze, and eye-related nonverbal communication. Eyes are said to be the window to the soul. - Through eye contact, one can tell if the other party is paying attention to the speaker's words. - It can also help in determining whether one is saying the truth or not. - Through eye contact we can be able to know one's emotional condition.

2. PROXEMICS Another notable area in the nonverbal world of body language is that of spatial relationships, which is also known as Proxemics. Introduced by Edward T. Hall in 1966, Proxemics is the study of measurable distances between people as they interact with one another. Hall also came up with four distinct zones in which most men operate: Intimate distance for embracing, touching or whispering Personal distance for interactions among good friends or family members Social distance for interactions among acquaintances Public Distance used for public speaking.

3. HAPTICS(Touch)- It is a subcategory of Body Language, and the study of touching as such, handshakes, holding hands, back slapping, high fives, brushing up against someone or patting someone all have meaning. Touching is the most developed sense at birth and formulates our initial views of the world. Touching can be used to sooth, for amusement during play, to flirt, to express power and maintain bonds between people, such as with baby and mother.

4. CHRONEMICS (Time)– The use of time in nonverbal communication is formally defined as chronemics. Time perceptions include punctuality, willingness to wait, and interactions. The use of time can affect lifestyles, daily agendas, speed of speech, movements and how long people are willing to listen.

5. PARALANGUAGE– The attributes of voice like audibility, pleasantness, distinctness, and correctness in pronunciation, flexibility, etc. help to shape the meaning in oral communication. - These attributes help in creating meaning. - Paralanguage goes beyond the linguistic form of an utterance. Diction, the highness and lowness of tone, intensity, the manner of delivery, rate of speaking, etc. create the intended meaning of an utterance. - When something is delivered coupled with gestures and facial expressions may reflect the feeling(s) and/or emotion(s) of the participant in a communicative situation.

6. APPEARANCE: Personal appearance refers to the way the audiences with their expectations of appropriateness, see and evaluate the way you look. The ways you look is all about your outward appearance of clothing, grooming, and make-ups. Physical appearance largely determines attractiveness and those who are attractive are more likely to be considered as more intelligent, more persuasive, and more likeable than the unattractive ones. Appearances also include:

- Hairstyles
- Body cleanliness
- Clean Nails
- Shiny shoes
- No tattoos
- Being appropriately dressed

7. ARTIFACTS: Artifacts are forms of decorative ornamentation that are chosen to represent self concept. They can include rings and tattoos, but may also include brand names and logos. From clothes to cars, watches, briefcases, purses, and even eyeglasses, what we choose to surround ourselves with communicates something about our sense of self. They may project gender, role or position, class or status, personality, and group membership or affiliation.

8. ENVIRONMENT: Environment involves the physical and psychological aspects of the communication context. The perception of one's environment influences one's reaction to it. For example, Google is famous for its work environment, with spaces created for physical activity and even in-house food service around the clock. The expense is no doubt considerable, but Google's actions speak volumes. The results produced in the environment, designed to facilitate creativity, interaction, and collaboration, are worth the effort.

Barriers To Communication:

The barrier of communication is such a part that you have to keep in mind during every communication. Even after taking care of every other detail during the conversation, some misunderstandings remain during communication. Therefore, we must keep in mind some communication barriers to eliminate misunderstandings. Barriers during communication can be of many types such as linguistic barriers, physical barriers, Personal barriers, Gender barriers, Emotional barriers, Language Barriers, Status Barriers, Cultural Barriers, Organizational Barriers, Semantic Barriers, and Inattention Barriers and many more barriers.

1. Physical Barriers: It is also caused by barrier distance. Suppose that the person sending the message is far away from the recipient. And communication is happening between the two. The barrier arises due to him not being heard clearly because of far distance.

2. Personal Barriers: The personal factors of both sender and receiver may exert influence on effective communication. These factors include life experiences, emotions, attitudes, behavior that hinders the ability of a person to communicate.

3. Gender barriers: Gender barrier is also a type of barrier, such as male and female in an organization, people of both genders work. Societal stereotypes, assumed gender roles, and interpersonal differences can contribute to a communication gap between the gender and there is a rift between people due to gender. For Example: Women are focused on relationships and men are focused on tasks.

4. Emotional Barriers: The emotional barrier changes according to our mood. Emotional barriers are due to mental limitations created by one's own self. Emotional Barriers are the mental walls that keep you from openly communicating your thoughts and feeling to others.

5. Language Barriers: Language barriers are the most common communication barriers which cause misunderstandings and misinterpretations between people. ... Not using the words that other person understands makes the communication ineffective and prevents message from being conveyed.

6. Status Barriers: People often have difficulty navigating status differences when trying to inform or persuade others. To many, social status is an indicator of credibility and legitimacy, and this effects how seriously others take what one communicates. Status differences can create a bias against those with the perceived lower status.

7. Cultural Barriers: Past experiences, perception, and cultural background greatly affect the way people talk and behave. Culture plays an important role in shaping the style of communication. ... The culture in which individuals are socialized influences the way they communicate, and the way individuals communicate can change the culture.

8. Organizational Barriers: Inside the organization, there are many things inside which a communication barrier is created. Just like the policy of the organization, about the rule and regulation of the organization, about the status, the facility, there are many other things which cause a lot of barriers.

9. Semantic Barriers: Semantic barriers to communication are the symbolic obstacles that distort the sent message in some other way than intended, making the message difficult to understand. The meaning of words, signs and symbols might be different from one person to another and the same word might have hundreds of meanings.

10. Inattention barriers: Sometime the persons do not pay adequate attention to the message. They do not listen, the spoken words attentively. The communication has no impact on those who are unwilling to listen. Inattention arises due to lack of interest, over stimulation and time pressure.

Techniques to Overcome Barriers of Communication

Eliminating differences in perception: Seek clarity: if we are unclear about expectations, assumptions, preferences or beliefs of another person in an interaction, confusion may arise. The key to overcoming perceptual barriers is asking questions to gain a sense of clarity and ensure that you and the other person are on the same page.

Use of Simple Language: Use of simple and clear words should be emphasized. Use of ambiguous words and jargons should be avoided. Reduction and elimination of noise levels: Noise is the main communication barrier which must be overcome on priority basis. It is essential to identify the source of noise and then eliminate that source.

Active Listening: Listen attentively and carefully. There is a difference between "listening" and· "hearing". Active listening means hearing with proper understanding of the message that is heard. By asking questions the speaker can ensure whether his/her message is understood or not by the receiver in the same terms as intended by the speaker.

Emotional State: During communication one should make effective use of body language. He/she· should not show their emotions while communication as the receiver might misinterpret the message being delivered. For example, if the conveyer of the message is in a bad mood then the receiver might think that the information being delivered is not good. Simple Organizational Structure: The organizational structure should not be complex. The number· of hierarchical levels should be optimum. There should be a ideal span of control within the organization. Simpler the organizational structure, more effective will be the communication.

Avoid Information Overload: The managers should know how to prioritize their work. They should not overload themselves with the work. They should spend quality time with their subordinates and should listen to their problems and feedbacks actively.

Give Constructive Feedback: Avoid giving negative feedback. The contents of the feedback might be negative, but it should be delivered constructively. Constructive feedback will lead to effective communication between the superior and subordinate.

Proper Media Selection: The managers should properly select the medium of communication. Simple messages should be conveyed orally, like: face to face interaction or meetings. Use of written means of communication should be encouraged for delivering complex messages. For significant messages reminders can be given by using written means of communication such as : Memos, Notices etc.

Flexibility in meeting the targets: For effective communication in an organization the managers should ensure that the individuals are meeting their targets timely without skipping the formal channels of communication. There should not be much pressure on employees to meet their targets.

Guidelines For Effective Communication:

Effective communication is a part and parcel of any successful organization. A communication should be free from barriers so as to be effective. Communication is a two way process where the message sent by the sender should be interpreted in the same terms by the recipient. The characteristics of effective communication are as follows:

1. Clarity of Purpose: The message to be delivered must be clear in the mind of sender. The person whom it is targeted and the aim of the message should be clear in the mind of the sender.

2. Completeness: The message delivered should not be incomplete. It should be supported by facts and observations. It should be well planned and organized. No assumptions should be made by the receiver.

3. Conciseness: The message should be concise. It should not include any unnecessary details. It should be short and complete.

4. Feedback: Whether the message sent by the sender is understood in same terms by the receiver or not can be judged by the feedback received. The feedback should be timely and in personal. It should be specific rather than general.

5. Empathy: Empathy with the listeners is essential for effective verbal communication. The speaker should step into the shoes of the listener and be sensitive to their needs and emotions. This way he can understand things from their perspective and make communication more effective.

6.Modify the message according to the audience: The information requirement by different people in the organization differs according to their needs. What is relevant to the middle level management might not be relevant to the top level of management. Use of jargons should be minimized because it might lead to misunderstanding and misinterpretations. The message should be modified according to the needs and requirements of the targeted audience.

7. Multiple Channels of communication: For effective communication multiple channels should be used as it increases the chances of clarity of message. The message is reinforced by using different channels and there are less chances of deformation of message.

8. Make effective use of Grapevine (informal channel of communication): The employees and managers should not always discourage grapevine. They should make effective use of grapevine. The managers can use grapevine to deliver formal messages and for identification of issues which are significant for the employees. The managers can get to know the problems faced by the employees and can work upon it.

II
Interpersonal relationship

Introduction

A relationship is an interpersonal process where two or more people interact with each other. We meet people in a variety of settings and share our experiences and develop a kind of relatedness. The basis for good inter-personal relationships is respect for human personality with an understanding of the problem of other person. Understanding leads to co-operation and trust, which brings in harmony and happiness, which is very significant in developing therapeutics relationship loina the patient.

Definition

"A healthy interpersonal relationships is one in which the individuals involved, experiences intimacy with each other while maintaining separate identities". According to Sullivan, 'intimacy' is characterized by sensitivity to needs of the other person and mutual validation of personal worth.

Interpersonal relationship is a series of interactions where one individual perceives the other individual as a human being.

Interpersonal relationships in nursing is a mutually significant experience, where both nurse and patient view each other as a unique human beings.

Mrs. Bimla Kapoor (1994) has defined nurse – patient relationship, "as an Interaction process in which the nurse fulfills her role by using her professional knowledge and skill in such a way that s/he is able to help the patient physically, socially and emotionally."

Characteristics of healthy relations:

- Open communication of feelings.
- Acceptances of other as a valued unique identity.
- Deep empathetic understanding.

Principles

Principles which are the one needs to apply in establishing and maintaining interpersonal relationships:

- Principles of recognition
- Principles of mutual understanding
- Principles of inculcation of common interests
- Principle of respect for human dignity
- Principle of personality development
- Principle of stimulation, motivation and encouragement
- Principle of incentives/rewards for good accomplishment
- Principle of honesty, punctuality and trust worthiness.

Nursing is considered as an interpersonal process, which is often therapeutic, in that people benefit from the interaction. Nursing is also a human relationship between the one who is in need of health services and the nurse who is trained and prepared to respond to the need in therapeutic manner. The characteristics of a therapeutic relationship may include the following:

Characteristics

1. **Geniuness:** The individual involved in relationship is an open, honest and sincere to himself and to the others. It is opposite to self-alienation where individual's real and

Concepts in Nursing spontaneous reactions to life are suppressed. Genuineness means the person says the same thing what S/he feels and not saying something different than what is feeling.

1. **Respect:** 'Caring', 'liking' and 'valuing' are other terms for respect. It is non possessive warmth or unconditional positive regard which does not depend upon other person's behaviour. The other person is regarded as a person of worth and is respected but this does not mean that we condone or accept all aspects of the individual's behaviour as desirable or likable. The behaviour is viewed as normal, natural and expected in a growth circumstances.

2. **Empathetic Understanding:** Empathy is an ability to enter into the life of another person and to perceive his or her current feeling accurately Rogers (1975) described it as "to sense the client's private world as if it were your own, but without loosing the 'as if' quality. A high degree of empathy is one of the potent factors in bringing about change and learning one of the most delicate and powerful way we have of using ourselves". One has to keep aside one's view and values to enter another's world without prejudice. Accurate empathy is important for creating an environment in which a person can grow towards wellness. 'Active listening' and 'creative listening' are other terms, used for empathetic understanding.

Empathy is of two types:

- Basic empathy
- Trained empathy.

Basic empathy is a natural ability of an individual to feel for others; and trained empathy is taught and learnt for helping others. The trained empathy can also be termed a professional or clinical empathy. Genuine and unconditional regard and empathetic understanding conveyed to the other individual gives him or her personhood or identity this leads to changing self-concept resulting in changed behaviour.

4. **Concreteness:** Use of specific terminology, rather than using of abstraction in the discussion of patient's feeling, experiences and behaviour. Concreteness helps. It is opposite to generalizing, categorizing, classifying and labeling thus avoids vagueness and ambiguity. Concreteness keeps one person's responses close to the feelings of the other person; fosters accuracy of understanding and can contribute to empathetic understanding. The level of concreteness vary during different phases of interpersonal relationships/nurse patient relationship. In orientation phase concreteness should be high this will contribute to empathetic understanding, while a low level concreteness may be required to facilitate through self-exploration. High level of concreteness is essential at the termination phase when patients are engaging in action. Genuineness, report, empathetic understanding and concreteness – facilitate the formation of therapeutic nurse patient relationship/ interpersonal relationship.

Phases of Nurse-Patient Relationship

- Kapoor, Bimla (1994) has identified four phases of Nurse-Patient Relationship:
- Pre-interaction Phase;

- Introductory or Orientation Phase;
- Working Phase;
- Termination Phase.

1. The Pre-interaction Phase begins when the nurse is assigned a patient to develop therapeutic relationship with him/her till she goes to the patient for interaction: The tasks are that nurse explores her/his own fears and anxiety; Sets objectives for interaction phase; Takes help of the clinical supervisor or co-workers to overcome the fears.
2. Introductory/Orientation Phase: It begins when the nurse goes to the patient and introduces herself/himself to the patient: The tasks are that the nurse introduces herself/himself to the patient; Talks with the patients.
3. Working Phase: Working phase of the nurse-patient relationship starts when the nurse and patient start interacting with each other and nurse collect the data from primary and secondary sources. Assists the patient to identify his/her problems, Plan the nursing intervention.
4. Termination Phase is also called as resolution phase. It begins with orientation phase itself when nurse explains to the patient the purpose of care to the patient. The tasks of nurse would be to help the client: To make best use of the services available; Get prepared for discharge; Get informed about rehabilitation and follow up.

Phases of Nurse-Patient Relationship

Orientation Phase

- This is the phase when patient and the nurse get to know each other. They start off as strangers. Though the nurse has the advantage of having some information about the patient through his records and from other nurses before she meets him.
- The nurse takes the initiative in the relationship by introducing herself to the patient and setting goals for working phase. In this phase security is been establish through continued development of trust. Patient is being assisted to verbalize thoughts and feelings while the strengths and weaknesses are being assessed.

Concepts in Nursing
Some time certain barriers appear such as the spoken language, manner in which nurse and patient perceive each other or anxiety of the both the participants in the interaction.

i. **Working Phase**

The working phase begins when nurse has collected all the information and begins to draw up a plan of care for the patient. In this the nurse and the patient develop mutually agreeable goals, and contract is formed, for example 'I shall demonstrate deep breathing exercises that you need to do before surgery. You need to practice them four times a day on your own so that you can perform them post operatively on your own.

During this phase nurse can take several therapeutic maneouvers. For Example: Offering support, remaining with the patient during stressful situation, helping the patient to arrive at his own decision and helping the patient to see his strengths, progress and successes. If the goals are met contract is terminated if not a new contract is negotiated.

Sometimes certain barrier can arise to accomplish the task–such as when patient starts testing the nurse or nurse's unwillingness to engage in the tedious task of improving her ability to collect and interpret data.

ii. **Termination Phase**

Termination is one of the most difficult but most critically important phases of nurse patient relationship. There are several reasons for termination of relationship such as when patient gets discharged or nurse's duty is transferred or when patient can manage his own health needs and care within reasonably safe limits or patient may be transferred to another ward or institution. Relationship can be for short duration or long duration, depends on the situation but feeling of loss is inevitable. This feeling one can overcome if the goals have been met and the patient no longer needs the nurse's care. We can review with the patient the accomplishments that have been made. Sometimes it is necessary that another person of your patient do this. In this case introduce the patient to the person who will be carrying for him. In case of transfer, prepare the patient for transfer. In larger hospitals,. A nurse is employed as discharge Co-coordinator and can assist in facilitating the discharge.

All the phases have action-oriented conditions which facilitate growth:

Based on the interpersonal theory of Peplau has also describe four phases of Nurse-Patient relationships. These are orientation, identification, exploitation and termination. One canvisualize an overlapping in all the phases

Orientation Phase:

- Nurse identifies patient's problems,
- Mutually formulate a contract

Identification Phase:

- Exchange social amenities;
- Nurse identifies patient's problems;
- Clarify each other's roles-nurse clarifies or correct the misconceptions on previous experience;

Exploitation Phase:

- Nurse and client start experiencing each other as unique individuals;
- Client experiences acceptance;
- Client develops high degree of trust in nurse;
- Client starts taking full advantage of the nurse Patient relationships;
- Client develops ability to test;

Termination Phase:

- Mutually explore feelings of rejection, loss, sadness and anger related behaviours;
- Client leans that termination that is important.
- Client learns that termination completes therapeutic relationships.

Role of A Nurse In Development of Interpersonal Relationship:
Role

- Stranger
- The roles assumed by both the nurse meeting;
- Resource person
- Provides knowledge and answers spec health Promotion;
- Surrogate
- Acts as substitute figure that the client i
- Teacher
- Identifies learning needs of the client a roles to develop clients interest in medi
- Leader
- Provides direction during present proble
- Socializing agent

- Participates in social activities with her
- Manager
- Establishes and maintains therapeutic conditions for patient's recovery;

Counselor

Facilitates self directed actions to help to changed life style.

Throughout the four phases of nurse patient relationship the nurse performs several roles. These are presented above in box no. 1 Peplau's theory is mainly concerned with the need for growth and development and with Psycho-social needs. Peplau's states that "the nursing process is educative and therapeutic when nurse and patient comes to know each other, as persons who are alike and yet, different, as persons who provided care and help in the solutions of problems". She states that Nursing is an interpersonal process that is often therapeutic and a force that promotes development of personality in becoming more creative and productive.

Factors Enhancing Interpersonal Relationships

Interpersonal factors refers to three factors involving relationships with others. The helpfulness of the support offered by others and satisfaction gained from it are critical to enhance good interpersonal-relationships, cooperation and mutual understanding between nurse and patient; nurse and nurse, nurse and doctor and nurse and patient's relative, are imperative to good interpersonal relationships. Co-operation and mutual understanding between all members of health team including patients are the basis of efficiency and is greatly influenced by the nurse in-charge of the unit. If interpersonal relations are good patients are well cared for and personal problems are reduced, concreteness in communication, immediacy in communication and sensitive confrontation is an important factor in establishing and maintaining good interpersonal relationships. The individual is helped when s/he is encouraged to express her/his concerns and willingness to clarify explicity. The most effective helper (nurse) does not avoid discussion about the dynamics (interaction) occurring within their relationship.

Nurse needs to develop some of the following characteristics which can help her establish good interpersonal relationships:

- Listen patiently
- Talk meaningfully
- Avoid hasty judgement
- Judge unemotionally
- Interpret properly
- Never gossip
- Never criticize
- Acquire adequate knowledge regarding the policy and administrative setup
- Know the other health agencies
- Acquire communication skills
- Respect others
- Accept constructive criticism
- Behave as human being towards patient (genuineness)
- Sensitive to point out discrepancies in patient's behaviour

Factors Leading To Poor Interpersonal Relationships

The following factors can lead to poor IPR:

- Lack of interest in work in some personnel may burden the other person which may spoil the friendly environment of the department.
- Lack of self-understanding and understanding of others is another factor leading to poor interpersonal relationship.

- Lack of understanding "how" you respond to others and what you expect from them.
- Deliberately ignoring some one without any cause is another factor leading to poor interpersonal relationships.
- Embarrassment for oneself and others from non-acceptance also contributes to poor interpersonal relationship.
- Unwilling to accept help and advice from others may also lead to unhealthy interpersonal relationships.
- There may be personality clash among people working in a unit. The clashes are usually caused by difference in styles of working.
- Conflicting ideas might arise from different backgrounds and lead to poor interpersonal relationships.

Role of A Nurse In Improving Interpersonal Relationships

In interpersonal relationship the nurse may use various methods to achieve good interpersonal relationships and these are definitely very important. Some of the methods are detailed below:

i. **Willingness to Give and Take:** You had an unhappy experience with a friend of yours in school time and started disliking her. In the hospital you meet a fellow nurse who resembles your old friend so you decide that you don't like her "type" and it seems you won't like her either. You work with her but she doesn't enjoy working with you. So she decides that she dislikes you. Your relationships are bound to be strained this made working environment tense and unhappy. All that needed here was willingness to accept your colleague as an individual, not as a "type". One nurse commented publically that she doesn't like Community Health Nurses (CHN) and she wouldn't work with the community people. Unfortunately she had to work in the community health field where nurses had very good IPR, which lead her to change her attitude towards CHNs. She was also able to establish good I.P.R. While working in the hospital you have many opportunities to please others by being willing to let them do you a favour, a favour which is perfectly acceptable from a professional point of view. Sometimes we can do a better job but we let others do it to please them.

A patient starts telling you some news from the newspaper, which you already know. If you want him to feel happy you will let him tell you the news. Healthy, enjoyable and good interpersonal relationships are possible among those individuals who understand the importance of unselfish acceptance and they believe in the principle of willingness to give and take. Be co-operative and appreciative with all your colleagues.

ii. **Acceptance of Others:** Nurses come in contact with a variety of people some attractive some are unattractive, aged, young, rich or poor. Keeping in mind the ethics and professional commitment nurse accept the fact that s/he need to give excellent care regardless of her/his own feelings. Nurse needs to overcome the feeling of distaste for anyone whose standard of personal appearance is different from her/his own.

To have satisfactory relationships with others in every situation we must accept that others have right to their habits as we have to ours. Exerting undue influence on anyone to change may not bring a long lasting improvement rather it may end up in a dislike for you and nothing else. While caring for a patient it is important to "accept him as he is". The nursing activities nurse undertake will become more rewarding and successful if the nurse hads developed rapport with the patient and 'accepting him as he is', is first step towards it. Through personal acquaintance one can get to know people better than just hearing about them or seeing them thus improves interpersonal relationships.

Respectful and healthy interpersonal relationships in the medical and nursing care of patients demand understanding and appreciation of special responsibilities each member of the health team has. Acceptance and co-operation leads to healthy and conducive atmosphere for congenial and productive working relationships.

iii. **Self Acceptance:** If we know or understand why we behave as we do in certain situations, will help us to understand the behaviour of others and adjust accordingly. Sometimes we feel glad to meet some one where as other time we will be inclined to wait for other person to take initiative. This happens with every one and it is normal. We must know what we do and why we do it, depends upon our familiarity to the environment, our status with our partner at that moment, duration and type of acquaintance with him/her. A professional nurse requires development in the socio-cultural aspects of life as well as in scientific and technological aspects. This is possible if the nurse sets some realistic and achievable goals for progress in all phases of nursing education.

iv. **Know-How:** 'It is very easy to preach but difficult to practice', well said by a wise man. "I want to adjust with others". "I want to get along well with others," "I want to give love to others and be loved by others," "I want to accept every one at any time in every situation". These are commonly expressed concerns of people, but how to go about

Concepts in Nursing

it is No definite steps to be followed which can be listed, however some suggestions can be of some use to the nurse:

- Courteous and respectful gesture to every one will be fruitful.
- Willingness to accept help and advice from others
- Communicate skillfully, avoid being argumentative and thrusting your opinions on others
- Keep the tone of voice and laughter under control.
- Get acquainted with all types of people
- Take advantage of time factor.
- Try to overcome your annoying and nervous habits, such as sniffing, finger tapping, whistling, continuous humming etc.
- Be careful of other people's possessions.
- Share appreciations with colleagues and other members of health team.
- Take your share of the blame in any situation.
- Should be generous and sincere in compliments.
- Try to clear up misunderstandings at the earliest.
- Be a modest looser and good winner.
- Avoid embarrassment for oneself and others.
- Indulging inspiteful gossip need to be evaded.
- Deliberately ignoring some one without good cause should be avoided.

v. **Emotional Maturity:** A mentally healthy person is enriched with emotions as s/he attains maturity and uses them intelligently. A nurse is considered to be mature person endowed with emotions. She can assess her present status in this respect and guide her progress ahead. Given below are some statements which can help you score you maturity level. An emotionally mature person is able to:

- Control her/his emotions in most situations.
- Use repression – a defense mechanism (what to forget and what to remember)
- Refuse to let easily hurt people, make him feel guilty and remorseful over trifles.
- Feel secure in the relationships with others.
- Expect to be liked, valued and accepts the facts which doesn't let it lead to lower the self-esteem.
- Carry on his work inspite of upsetting personal circumstances.
- Recognize his own need as well as others needs.
- Adjust to wide range of personalities without being emotionally involved.
- Keep his religious life in proper perspective.
- Refrain from being judgemental on emotional basis.

The Nurse and Her Patients:

The first responsibility of the nurse is to establishes rapport with her patient as she plans comprehensive care for him. The patient also carries some responsibility unless s/he is mentally sick or acutely ill physically. A sense of humour, infinite patience and dignity will help the nurse to earn respect and liking from her patient and keep her relationship as a professional one.

Therapeutic relationships with patients who are fearful, shy, unsure of themselves can help them express their needs. Warm professional atmosphere conducive for patients' recovery can be achieved through good interpersonal relationships at the unit.

Johari Window

Background

The Johari Window model was developed by American psychologists Joseph Luft and Harry Ingham in the 1950's. The Johari Window soon became a commonly used model for understanding and training self-awareness, individual development, recuperating communications, interpersonal relationships, group dynamics, team development and inter-group relationships. The Johari Window model is also known as a 'Disclosure or Feedback model of self awareness' and also 'Information Processing Tool'. The Johari Window essentially signifies information - feelings, knowledge, views, attitudes, skills, intentions, motivation etc within or about a person - in relation to their group, from four viewpoints, which are discussed below (See figure 1). Johari Window refers to 'Self' and 'Others'. 'Self' means oneself and 'Others' means other person in the person's group.

The quadrants are basically divided in four categories:

- Open area - what you know about yourself and others also know
- Blind area - what you don't know about yourself but others do know
- Hidden area - what you know about yourself but others don't know
- Unknown area - what neither you nor others know about you.

The quadrants inflate or contract in relation to each other as you achieve more knowledge about yourself through experience, surveillance, feedback from others, communication, self reflection etc. To work most efficiently and effectively, one need to develop an 'open' area of him/her. This is the space where communication is good with no misapprehension as there is openness. Learning more about yourself through a new situation, such as work experience, can shrivel your 'Unknown' area and enlarge your 'Hidden' area. If you converse this self learning to other people, you enlarge your 'open' area, where people discern you and you know yourself. If you ask for feedback, then people know about you will become part of yourself knowledge, stirring from your 'blind' area to 'open' area.

Four regions of Johari Window

The four Johari Window viewpoints are known 'regions' or 'quadrants'. Each of these regions symbolizes the information, feelings, motivation etc in terms of whether the information is known or unknown by the person, and whether the information is known or unknown by others in the group.

The Johari Window's four regions are ARENA, FACADE, BLINDSPOT, and UNKNOWN What is known by the person about him/herself and is also known by others is Open Area or 'The Arena'. What is unknown by the person about him/herself but which others know is Blind Area or 'Blindspot'. What the person knows about him/herself that others do not know is known as Hidden Area or 'Facade'. What is unknown by the person about him/herself and is also unknown by others is Unknown self.

Johari Region 1

Johari region 1 is also acknowledged as the 'Area of Free Activity'. It contains information about the person - conduct, thoughts, feelings, sentiment, awareness, experience, skills, views etc known by the person himself/herself and known by the others. The intend of any group should be to extend the 'Open Area' for each person, since when we work with others in this area we are at our most efficient and productive. The open free area is also known as ' Arena' which can be seen. as the space where excellent communications and cooperation crop up, free from interruption, doubt, puzzlement, clash and misapprehension. Reputable team members rationally tend to have generously proportioned open areas than new team members. Fresh team members start with comparatively small open areas as reasonably little knowledge about the new team member is shared. The size of the open area can be stretched horizontally into the Blind space, by seeking and vigorously listening to feedback from other group members. This course of action is known as 'Feedback Solicitation'. The size of the open area can also be stretched vertically downwards into the Hidden Space by the person's confession of information, feelings, etc about him/herself to the group and its members. Group members can facilitate a person inflate their open area into the Hidden area by asking the person about him/herself. Managers and team leaders can play a significant role in facilitating feedback and revelation among group members, and in unswervingly giving feedback to individuals about their own Blind areas. Leaders also have a huge responsibility to endorse a culture and expectation for open, truthful, constructive, supportive, productive, sensitive communications, and the sharing of knowledge throughout their group. Top performing groups, departments, companies and organizations constantly tend to have a culture of open encouraging communication, so encouraging the positive development of the 'open area' or 'open self' for everyone is effortless yet elementary facet of successful leadership.

Johari Region 2

Johari region 2 is what is known about a person by others in the group, but is unknown by the person him/herself. It is known as Blind Area. By soliciting feedback from others, the endeavour should be to condense this area and thus to increase the open area, i.e. to augment self-awareness. This blind area is not an effective space for individuals or groups. This blind area could also be referred to as unawareness about oneself, or issues in which one is deceived. A blind area could also embrace issues that others are intentionally withholding from a person. We all know how complicated it is to work well when kept in the dim. Group members and managers can take some duty for helping an individual to trim down their blind area - in turn mounting the open area - by giving susceptible feedback and cheering disclosure. Managers should encourage a climate of non-judgmental feedback, and group retort to individual disclosure, which shrinks fear and consequently promotes both processes to ensue. The level to which an individual seeks feedback, and the issues on which feedback is hunted, must always be at the individual's own prudence. Some people are suppler than others - care needs to be taken to shun emotional upset.

Johari Region 3

Johari region 3 is what is known to us but kept reserved or hidden from others and hence unknown, to others. This hidden or avoided self signifies information, feelings, etc, anything that a person knows about self, but which is not exposed to others. The Hidden area could also embrace sensitivities, qualms, hidden agendas, scheming intentions, and secrets - anything that a person knows but does not divulge, for whatever motive. It's natural for very own and privateinformation and feelings to remain secreted, certainly, certain information, feelings and experiences have no bearing onwork, and should remain hidden. Conversely, a lot of hidden information is not very personal, it is work-related, and so is better situated in the open area. Pertinent hidden information and feelings, etc, should be moved into the open area through the process of revelation. The aim should be to disclose and expose significant information and feelings - therefore the Johari Window terminology 'self-disclosure' and 'exposure process', thus escalating the open area. By telling others how we feel about ourselves reduces the hidden area, and amplify the open area, which facilitates better understanding, assistance, faith, team-working efficiency and productivity. Reducing hidden areas also lessen the potential for perplexity, misunderstanding, poor communication, etc, which undermine team effectiveness.

Johari Region 4

Johari region 4 enclose information, feelings, dormant abilities, aptitudes, experiences etc, that are unknown to the person him/herself and unknown to others in the group. These unknown subject take a multiplicity of forms: they can be feelings, behaviours, attitudes, ability, aptitudes, which can be fairly close to the surface, and which can be constructive and helpful, or they can be deeper facets of a person's individuality, swaying his/her behaviour to various degrees. Large unknown areas would classically be predictable in younger people who lack experience or self-belief. The unknown area could also embrace subconscious feelings rooted in influential events and shocking past experiences, which can stay unknown for a life span. In a work or organizational context the Johari Window should not be used to tackle issues of a clinical nature.

Principles of change within the Johari Window

Principles of Change within The Johari Window are discussed below:

- A transformation in any one quadrant will influence all other quadrants. Threat tends to dwindle awareness; mutual trust tends to amplify awareness.
- Forced awareness is detrimental and typically unsuccessful.
- Interpersonal learning means a revolution has taken place so that Quadrant I is larger, and one or more of the other quadrants has grown slighter.
- Working with others is assisted by a large sufficient area of free activity. This means additional of the resources and skills in the membership can be applied to the task.
- The lesser the first quadrant, the shoddier the communication.
- There is universal oddity about the unknown area; but this is held in check by custom, social training, and by varied fears.
- Sensitivity means appreciating the concealed facets of behaviour, in Quadrants II. III. IV and respecting the aspirations of others to keep them so.

The value system of a group and its membership may be noted in the way unknowns in the life of the group are brazen out.

Summary

- The Johari Window model was developed by American psychologists Joseph Luft and Harry Ingham in the 1950's.
- The Johari Window soon became an extensively used model for understanding and training self-awareness, personal development, recuperating communications, interpersonal relationships, group dynamics, team development and inter-group relationships.
- The Johari Window's four regions are ARENA, FACADE, BLINDSPOT, and UNKNOWN. These quadrants are also known as - open area, blindspot, hidden area and unknown area.
- Johari region 1 is also acknowledged as the 'Area of Free Activity'. It contains information about the person - conduct, thoughts, feelings, sentiment, awareness, experience, skills, views etc known by the person himself/ herself and known by the others.
- Johari region 2 is what is known about a person by others in the group, but is unknown by the person him/herself. It is known as Blind Area.

- Johari region 3 is what is known to us but kept reserved or hidden from others and hence unknown, to others. This hidden or avoided self signifies information, feelings, etc, anything that a person knows about self, but which is not exposed to others.
- Johari region 4 enclose information, feelings, dormant abilities, aptitudes, experiences etc, that are unknown to the person him/herself and unknown to others in the group.
- There are certain principles also within the Johari Window which are discussed above.

III

Human relation

Concept of Human relation

Human relation in nursing   a very significant aspect. The nurse is dealing with the human beings who have complex needs. They have their identity, life style, status and background. When they fall sick and are dependent on others for care, they need to be considered as unique human being. Nurse and the hospital team need to use effective communication skills so that the patient feels that they are being considered as an individual and not merely another patient suffering from a particular disease.

INTRODUCTION

Human relations are fundamental in a civil society & in each profession.

Nurses are one of the largest groups in health care workforce health care workforce & are constantly interacting with patients, their relatives, colleagues as well as other members of the multidisciplinary health care team inside & outside the health care organization.

DEFINITIONS OF HUMAN RELATIONS

Human relation is an area of management practice which is concerned with the integration of people into a work situation in a way that motivate them to work productively, cooperatively & with economic, psychological cooperatively & with economic, psychological & social satisfaction. Human relations are the relations between

Keith Davis

human being that are affected by many other factors & helps in the accomplishment of goals of an organization.

HUMAN RELATIONS IN NURSING

- Human relation in nursing refer to the relationship of nurses with colleagues & other department personnel & of nurses with patient.
- It is interdepartmental, interdepartmental & interpersonal relationship to provide the interpersonal relationship to provide the quality care to their patients.
- Human relations in nursing also develop when two health care personnel interact with each other to achieve the primary goal of maximum patient satisfaction & health promotion irrespective of their field of work

Dimensions of human relations in nursing

1. Nurse-patient helping relationships
2. Nurse-family relationships
3. Nurse community relationships
4. Nurse health team relationships

1. **Nurse-patient helping relationship**...

- Helping relationships are the foundations of clinical nursing practice.
- The nurse assumes the role of a professional helper in such relationships & comes to know patient's health needs.
- The nurse's therapeutic use of communication helps patients overcome their problems by achieving optimum health.
- In therapeutic relationships, nurse often encourage patients to share personal stories, which are called narrative interactions.

1. **Nurse-family relationships...**

- Many nursing situations, especially those in community & home care setting, require the nurse to form helping relationships with the patient's entire family.
- The same principles that guide one-to-one helping relationships also apply when the patient is a family unit, communication within families requires additional understanding of the complexities of family dynamics, needs & relationships.

3. **Nurse-health team relationships...**

- A nurse's functions or roles require interaction with multiple health team members. Communication in such relationships may be geared towards team building, facilitating the group process, collaboration, consultation, delegation, supervision, leadership & management.
- Both social as well as therapeutic interactions are needed between the nurse & health team members to build morale & strengthen relationships within the work setting.

4. **Nurse-community relationships...**

- Many nurses from relationships with community groups by participating in local organizations, volunteering for community service or by becoming politically active nurses in a community-based practice. They must be able to establish relationships with their community to be effective change agents.
- Communication within the community take place through channels such as neighborhood, newsletters, public bulletin boards, newspapers, radio, television & electronic information sites.

Self concept

- Self-concept is a person's understanding of how & what someone thinks about him orher.
- Understanding the self is the ability tounderstand one's own thoughts & actions.
- It is a subjective sense of the self & a complex mixture of unconscious & conscious thoughts, attitudes & perceptions.

Components of self- concept

- Body image
- Personal identity
- Self esteem
- Role performance

Definition of understanding Self

Self Understanding self represents the sum total of people's conscious perception of their identity as distinct from others. It is not a static phenomenon, but continues to develop & change throughout our lives. –

George Herbert Head

The understanding self is thinking about what is involved in being? What distinguish you from being an object, an animal or different person?

- Richard Stevens

Importance of understanding self

Self-understanding has been recognized as a key competency for individuals to function efficiently organizations. It influences an individual's ability to makekey decisions about self, others around & organizations.

Understanding the self equips individuals with making more effective career & lifechoice, the ability to lead, guide & inspirewith authenticity resulting in significantlyimproved organizational productivity.

Johari window: A tool to understanding self

The Johari window, created by Joseph Luft & Harry Ingham, is a useful tool for providing self-explanation.

The four panes of the Johari window represents the four parts of our self. The public self, the hidden self, blindspot & the unconscious self.

Strategies to improve self understanding

- To increase the size of the open window vertically downwards into the hidden space, one can disclose his or her personal information, feelings, etc., to the team members.
- The unknown area can be reduced by other's observation, self discovery or mutual enlightenment via group experiences & discussion.
- The blind self is not an effective space for individuals or groups so it needs to be diminished. This can be done by seeking or soliciting feedback from others thereby increasing the open area.
- The hidden window must always be at the individual's own discretion.

Social Behaviour

- The interaction that takes between members of the same species or the behavior directed towards the society is known as social behavior.
- In a sociological hierarchy, social behavior is followed by social actions, is directed at other people & designed to provoke a response.
- Antisocial behavior refers to behavior that may cause harm to the society.

Types of social behavior

- Aggression
- Social behavior
- Altruism
- Shyness
- Scapegoating

1. **Aggression**

- It refers to the behavior between members of the same species with an intention to hurt, ridicule or humiliate the other person.
- Aggression can be displayed in many ways in humans & can be physical, psychological or verbal.

2. **Altruism**

- It refers to feeling of concern, sympathy & benevolence for others.

- It is a traditional virtue in some cultures or can be an inbuilt part of religious expectations that the followers feel motivated for.
- Pure altruism is an inconsideration for any rewards or direct or indirect benefit with no expectation of any compensation.

3. Scapegoating

- It is the practice of isolation of any partyfor derogatory or negative treatment or blame.
- It is the process where the mechanism of projection or displacement are utilized in directing feelings of aggression, hostility, frustration, etc. upon another individual or group, with the amount of blame being unwarranted.

4. Shyness

- It is a feeling of discomfort, nervousness, lack of confidence or awkwardness when a person is in the proximity (especially ina situation where one has to deal with) of an unfamiliar person.
- Shyness can originate from genetic traits or the upbringing & personality type.

Factors influencing social behavior

Social Attitude

- Attitude is the state of conscious within the individual human being.
- It refers to certain regularities of an individual's feelings, thoughts & predisposition to act towards some aspects of his environment.
- Social attitude refers to how a group of people or individuals from a society perceive other objects, situations, people & phenomenon.
- Example, some individual may have negative social attitude with HIV patient

Definition of social attitude

Attitude is the sum total of a man's inclination & feelings, prejudices or bias, preconceived notions, ideas, fear, threats & conviction about any specific topic.

-Thurstone

Attitude is a state of mind of the individual towards a value that may be love of money, desire for fame, appreciation for God.

-Thomas

Importance of social attitude

- Social attitude determines the social behavior of a person.
- It provides a mechanism of social control.
- Life organization demands membership in a group & attitudes are an expression of the desire for status.
- Approval or acceptance of an individual's behavior reinforces social behavior.
- Social rejection of an activity restraints the culprit from repeating the same activity in future thus maintaining conformity.

Changes in social attitude attitude

- It is dynamic attribute that keeps on changing with new experiences. A change in social could be positive & negative.
- Alteration in attitudes do not arrive alone; they come hand-in-hand with changed social values.
- A sudden change involve a radical modification of many attitudes is commonly known as a conversation. It is a sudden withdrawal fromone's usual attitude to adjust to new needs.

Motivation

- Motivation is derived from the Latin word movere which means "to move" or "to energize" or " to activate."
- It is a process that produces energy or drive in the individual to proceed with an activity.
- The activity is aroused, fulfills the need & reduces the drive of tension.
- Motivation is often used to refer to an individual's goals, needs, wants &intentions.

Definitions of motivation

Motivation is the process of arousing the action, sustaining the activity in process ®ulating the pattern of activity.

-Young

Motivating refers to the states within a person or animal that drives behavior toward some goal.

-Morgan & king

Motivational approach

1. **Be-strong approach**

- Conventionally, the management resorted to being strong.
- According to this approach, the enterprise put a thrust on economic rewards.
- The assumption was that people work more efficiently if threatened with financial loss or penalty on failure to do their job.

2. **Be-good/paternalistic approach**

- The be-good approach refers to rewarding personnel to get productive work in return. Rewards may include job security, recreation, fair supervision & sound working condition.

3. **Effort reward approach**

- This approach operates on the basis of the effort or endeavor on the part of personnel to achieve organizational objectives.
- The manager sets up standards of practice & observes adherence to these standards. Ultimately, the reward is decided on the basis of performance. This gives a sense of motivation to work.

Maslow's priority model of motivation

Individual And Groups

- An individual is a single unit in a group & a group is a collection of many individuals with a common purpose.
- Individuals & groups are reciprocal to each other because without individuals groups cannot be formed & individuals have no existence or cannot meet their physical, psychological, social & spiritual needs without groups of other individuals.

Definition of group

A social group is a give aggregate of people, playing inter-related roles & recognized by themselves or others as a unit of interaction.

-Williams

Characteristics of a group

- Each group has its own identity & structure.
- A group includes at least two or more people.
- Group members have a shared purpose or goal.
- Group members have a conscious identification with each other.
- Group members need each other's help to accomplish the purposes for which they have organize.
- Group members influence, interact with each other.
- Every group has its own rules & norms members are supposed to follow.

Classification of groups

- Dwight Sanderson classification of social groups by structure.

  - Involuntary group
  - Voluntary group
  - Delegate group

- Charles Cooley classification

  - Primary group
  - Secondary group

- George hasen classification of groups on the basis of their relationship with other groups.

  - Unsocial group
  - Pseudosocial group
  - Rama Universi Pseudosocial group
  - Prof Sudharani 41 Antisocial group
  - Prosocial group

Tasks or roles of an individual in a group

- Initiator
- Information seeker
- Information giver
- Opinion seeker Elaborator
- Coordinator
- Orienteer Evaluator
- Energizer
- Procedural technician Recorder
- Group-building
- & maintenance roles

Group Dynamics

- Kurt Lewin, a social psychologist at the University of Lowa, USA, was the creatorof the term group dynamics.
- Group dynamics is the study of groups & also a general term for a group process.
- In organizational development or group dynamics, the phrase group process refers to an insight into the behavior of group members & to incline their behaviors towards the achievement of group goals.

Meaning of group dynamics

- Group dynamics is the study of activities or processes that are responsible for various group phenomena.
- Group dynamics is the study of group interstimulation & invoking of response between individuals to perform various group phenomena.

Aspects of group discipline

- Formation of group
- Group task
- Composition of group
- Communication between group members
- Mode of working relationships between members of a group
- Growth, downfall &resolution
- Method to achieve oneness
- Group dissolution of the group & building consensus
- Task performance
- Acclimatization to meet the needs of the group

Stages of group development

1. Forming phase
2. Storming phase
3. Norming phase
4. Performing phase

Stages of group development

Strategies to improve group functioning

- Individuals participating in a group must have a clear understanding of individual goals as well as group objectives so that their interaction is goal oriented.
- People participating in a group must have a clear idea about expectations within a group
- Group members must have a clear. understanding of their responsibilities & should be committed towards their designated responsibilities.
- Members in a group must follow the principles of positive competence.
- Appropriate control over the functioning of group members must be maintained.
- The group members must carry out their— functions with a collaborative approach.
- Group members must communicate effectively & appropriately for a group to function smoothly.
- A group leader must coordinate individual tasks to obtain group objectives.

Teamwork

- Teamwork divides the task & multiple the success.
- Teamwork is an action performed by a team towards a common goal.
- A team consists of more than one person, & each person typically has different responsibilities.
- Teamwork leads to personal recognition, raises self-esteem & increases motivation & commitment.

Elements of a team

- Common purpose
- Interdependence
- Clarity of roles & contribution
- Satisfaction from working together
- Mutual & individual accountability
- Realization of synergies
- Empowerment

Health team

- The quality of health & medical care is best if professional groups like physicians, nurses, paramedical workers, health educators, health visitors, public health engineers & many others share a common unifying goal.
- Teamwork can be defined as a dynamic process involving two or more two or more health care professionals with complementary background & skills, sharing common health goals & exercising concerted physical & mental effort in assessing, planning or evaluating patient care in health.

care.
Functional classification of teams
Health care team:
It consists of all those who are involved in improving a community health setting without necessarily being in contact with patients actively.
Medical care team:
It consists of professionals & paraprofessionals that provide services for community health provide services for patients, generally in a hospital setting, without any direct or personal contact with them.
Patient care team:
It comprises any group of professionals & semiprofessionals in a hospital setting who jointly provide services that bring them in direct contact with patients.
Advantages of teamwork

- It gives a better end result with high-quality performance from each team member.
- It involve every person & his expertise & responsibilities.
- The execution of new ideas can be more effective & efficient through teamwork.
- It increase ownership with wider communication.
- It leads to information sharing & increases learning in the team & the organization.
- It provide more security & develops personal relationships.
- A particular problem can easily solved in team.
- It helps provide a variety of solutions.
- It increases the willingness of every member to take more risk.
- A team can handle more difficult & complex problem in the workplace.
- A team increases the accuracy of problem solving

Disadvantages of teamwork

- It may lead to unequal participation of members in a team.
- Some individuals may be good workers,they may not be good team payers.
- It may limit creative thinking
- A team can sometimes take longer to produce desire results.
- **Concept of Human relation**

  Human relation in nursing   a very significant aspect. The nurse is dealing with the human beings who have complex needs. They have their identity, life style, status and background. When they fall sick and are dependent on others for care, they need to be considered as unique human being. Nurse and the hospital team need to use effective communication skills so that the patient feels that they are being considered as an individual and not merely another patient suffering from a particular disease.

  INTRODUCTION

  Human relations are fundamental in a civil society & in each profession.

  Nurses are one of the largest groups in health care workforce health care workforce & are constantly interacting with patients, their relatives, colleagues as well as other members of the multidisciplinary health care team inside & outside the health care organization.

  DEFINITIONS OF HUMAN RELATIONS

  Human relation is an area of management practice which is concerned with the integration of people into a work situation in a way that motivate them to work productively, cooperatively & with economic, psychological cooperatively & with economic, psychological & social satisfaction. Human relations are the relations between

  Keith Davis

  human being that are affected by many other factors & helps in the accomplishment of goals of an organization.

  HUMAN RELATIONS IN NURSING
- Human relation in nursing refer to the relationship of nurses with colleagues & other department personnel & of nurses with patient.
- It is interdepartmental, interdepartmental & interpersonal relationship to provide the interpersonal relationship to provide the quality care to their patients.
- Human relations in nursing also develop when two health care personnel interact with each other to achieve the primary goal of maximum patient satisfaction & health promotion irrespective of their field of work
- Dimensions of human relations in nursing
- Nurse-patient helping relationships
- Nurse-family relationships
- Nurse community relationships
- Nurse health team relationships

- **Nurse-patient helping relationship...**
- Helping relationships are the foundations of clinical nursing practice.
- The nurse assumes the role of a professional helper in such relationships & comes to know patient's health needs.
- The nurse's therapeutic use of communication helps patients overcome their problems by achieving optimum health.
- In therapeutic relationships, nurse often encourage patients to share personal stories, which are called narrative interactions.
- **Nurse-family relationships...**
- Many nursing situations, especially those in community & home care setting, require the nurse to form helping relationships with the patient's entire family.
- The same principles that guide one-to-one helping relationships also apply when the patient is a family unit, communication within families requires additional understanding of the complexities of family dynamics, needs & relationships.
- **Nurse-health team relationships...**
- A nurse's functions or roles require interaction with multiple health team members. Communication in such relationships may be geared towards team building, facilitating the group process, collaboration, consultation, delegation, supervision, leadership & management.
- Both social as well as therapeutic interactions are needed between the nurse & health team members to build morale & strengthen relationships within the work setting.
- **Nurse-community relationships...**
- Many nurses from relationships with community groups by participating in local organizations, volunteering for community service or by becoming politically active nurses in a community-based practice. They must be able to establish relationships with their community to be effective change agents.
- Communication within the community take place through channels such as neighborhood, newsletters, public bulletin boards, newspapers, radio, television & electronic information sites.
- **Self concept**
- Self-concept is a person's understanding of how & what someone thinks about him orher.
- Understanding the self is the ability tounderstand one's own thoughts & actions.
- It is a subjective sense of the self & a complex mixture of unconscious & conscious thoughts, attitudes & perceptions.
- **Components of self- concept**
- Body image
- Personal identity
- Self esteem
- Role performance
- **Definition of understanding Self**

    Self Understanding self represents the sum total of people's conscious perception of their identity as distinct from others. It is not a static phenomenon, but continues to develop & change throughout our lives. –

    George Herbert Head

    The understanding self is thinking about what is involved in being? What distinguish you from being an object, an animal or different person?

    - Richard Stevens

    Importance of understanding self

    Self-understanding has been recognized as a key competency for individuals to function efficiently organizations. It influences an individual's ability to makekey decisions about self, others around & organizations.

    Understanding the self equips individuals with making more effective career & lifechoice, the ability to lead, guide & inspirewith authenticity resulting in significantlyimproved organizational productivity.

    Johari window: A tool to understanding self

The Johari window, created by Joseph Luft & Harry Ingham, is a useful tool for providing self-explanation.

The four panes of the Johari window represents the four parts of our self. The public self, the hidden self, blindspot & the unconscious self.

Strategies to improve self understanding

- To increase the size of the open window vertically downwards into the hidden space, one can disclose his or her personal information, feelings, etc., to the team members.
- The unknown area can be reduced by other's observation, self discovery or mutual enlightenment via group experiences & discussion.
- The blind self is not an effective space for individuals or groups so it needs to be diminished. This can be done by seeking or soliciting feedback from others thereby increasing the open area.
- The hidden window must always be at the individual's own discretion.

Social Behaviour

- The interaction that takes between members of the same species or the behavior directed towards the society is known as social behavior.
- In a sociological hierarchy, social behavior is followed by social actions, is directed at other people & designed to provoke a response.
- Antisocial behavior refers to behavior that may cause harm to the society.

Types of social behavior

- Aggression
- Social behavior
- Altruism
- Shyness
- Scapegoating

Aggression

- It refers to the behavior between members of the same species with an intention to hurt, ridicule or humiliate the other person.
- Aggression can be displayed in many ways in humans & can be physical, psychological or verbal.

Altruism

- It refers to feeling of concern, sympathy & benevolence for others.
- It is a traditional virtue in some cultures or can be an inbuilt part of religious expectations that the followers feel motivated for.
- Pure altruism is an inconsideration for any rewards or direct or indirect benefit with no expectation of any compensation.

Scapegoating

- It is the practice of isolation of any partyfor derogatory or negative treatment or blame.
- It is the process where the mechanism of projection or displacement are utilized in directing feelings of aggression, hostility, frustration, etc. upon another individual or group, with the amount of blame being unwarranted.

Shyness

- It is a feeling of discomfort, nervousness, lack of confidence or awkwardness when a person is in the proximity (especially ina situation where one has to deal with) of an unfamiliar person.
- Shyness can originate from genetic traits or the upbringing & personality type.

Factors influencing social behavior

Social Attitude

- Attitude is the state of conscious within the individual human being.
- It refers to certain regularities of an individual's feelings, thoughts & predisposition to act towards some aspects of his environment.
- Social attitude refers to how a group of people or individuals from a society perceive other objects, situations, people & phenomenon.
- Example, some individual may have negative social attitude with HIV patient

Definition of social attitude

Attitude is the sum total of a man's inclination & feelings, prejudices or bias, preconceived notions, ideas, fear, threats & conviction about any specific topic.

-Thurstone

Attitude is a state of mind of the individual towards a value that may be love of money, desire for fame, appreciation for God.

-Thomas

Importance of social attitude

- Social attitude determines the social behavior of a person.
- It provides a mechanism of social control.
- Life organization demands membership in a group & attitudes are an expression of the desire for status.
- Approval or acceptance of an individual's behavior reinforces social behavior.
- Social rejection of an activity restraints the culprit from repeating the same activity in future thus maintaining conformity.

Changes in social attitude attitude

- It is dynamic attribute that keeps on changing with new experiences. A change in social could be positive & negative.
- Alteration in attitudes do not arrive alone; they come hand-in-hand with changed social values.
- A sudden change involve a radical modification of many attitudes is commonly known as a conversation. It is a sudden withdrawal fromone's usual attitude to adjust to new needs.

Motivation

- Motivation is derived from the Latin word movere which means "to move" or "to energize" or " to activate."

- It is a process that produces energy or drive in the individual to proceed with an activity.
- The activity is aroused, fulfills the need & reduces the drive of tension.
- Motivation is often used to refer to an individual's goals, needs, wants &intentions.
- **Definitions of motivation**

  Motivation is the process of arousing the action, sustaining the activity in process ®ulating the pattern of activity.

  -Young

  Motivating refers to the states within a person or animal that drives behavior toward some goal.

  -Morgan & king

  Motivational approach
- **Be-strong approach**
- Conventionally, the management resorted to being strong.
- According to this approach, the enterprise put a thrust on economic rewards.
- The assumption was that people work more efficiently if threatened with financial loss or penalty on failure to do
- their job.
- **Be-good/paternalistic approach**
- The be-good approach refers to rewarding personnel to get productive work in return. Rewards may include job
- security, recreation, fair supervision & sound working condition.
- **Effort reward approach**
- This approach operates on the basis of the effort or endeavor on the part of personnel to achieve organizational objectives.
- The manager sets up standards of practice & observes adherence to these standards. Ultimately, the reward is decided on the basis of performance. This gives a sense of motivation to work.
- **Maslow's priority model of motivation**

Individual And Groups

- An individual is a single unit in a group & a group is a collection of many individuals with a common purpose.
- Individuals & groups are reciprocal to each other because without individuals groups cannot be formed & individuals have no existence or cannot meet their physical, psychological, social & spiritual needs without groups of other individuals.

Definition of group

A social group is a give aggregate of people, playing inter-related roles & recognized by themselves or others as a unit of interaction.

-Williams

Characteristics of a group

- Each group has its own identity & structure.
- A group includes at least two or more people.
- Group members have a shared purpose or goal.
- Group members have a conscious identification with each other.
- Group members need each other's help to accomplish the purposes for which they have organize.
- Group members influence, interact with each other.
- Every group has its own rules & norms members are supposed to follow.

Classification of groups

- Dwight Sanderson classification of social groups by structure.

  - Involuntary group
  - Voluntary group
  - Delegate group

- Charles Cooley classification

  - Primary group
  - Secondary group

- George hasen classification of groups on the basis of their relationship with other groups.

  - Unsocial group
  - Pseudosocial group
  - Rama Universi Pseudosocial group
  - Prof Sudharani 41 Antisocial group
  - Prosocial group

- **Tasks or roles of an individual in a group**
- Initiator
- Information seeker
- Information giver
- Opinion seeker Elaborator
- Coordinator
- Orienteer Evaluator
- Energizer
- Procedural technician Recorder
- Group-building
- & maintenance roles
- **Group Dynamics**
- Kurt Lewin, a social psychologist at the University of Lowa, USA, was the creatorof the term group dynamics.
- Group dynamics is the study of groups & also a general term for a group process.
- In organizational development or group dynamics, the phrase group process refers to an insight into the behavior of group members & to incline their behaviors towards the achievement of group goals.
- **Meaning of group dynamics**
- Group dynamics is the study of activities or processes that are responsible for various group phenomena.
- Group dynamics is the study of group interstimulation & invoking of response between individuals to perform various group phenomena.
- **Aspects of group discipline**
- Formation of group
- Group task
- Composition of group
- Communication between group members
- Mode of working relationships between members of a group
- Growth, downfall &resolution
- Method to achieve oneness
- Group dissolution of the group & building consensus
- Task performance
- Acclimatization to meet the needs of the group
- **Stages of group development**
- Forming phase
- Storming phase
- Norming phase

- Performing phase
- **Stages of group development**

Strategies to improve group functioning
- Individuals participating in a group must have a clear understanding of individual goals as well as group objectives so that their interaction is goal oriented.
- People participating in a group must have a clear idea about expectations within a group
- Group members must have a clear. understanding of their responsibilities & should be committed towards their designated responsibilities.
- Members in a group must follow the principles of positive competence.
- Appropriate control over the functioning of group members must be maintained.
- The group members must carry out their— functions with a collaborative approach.
- Group members must communicate effectively & appropriately for a group to function smoothly.
- A group leader must coordinate individual tasks to obtain group objectives.
- **Teamwork**
- Teamwork divides the task & multiple the success.
- Teamwork is an action performed by a team towards a common goal.
- A team consists of more than one person, & each person typically has different responsibilities.
- Teamwork leads to personal recognition, raises self-esteem & increases motivation & commitment.
- **Elements of a team**
- Common purpose
- Interdependence
- Clarity of roles & contribution
- Satisfaction from working together
- Mutual & individual accountability
- Realization of synergies
- Empowerment
- **Health team**
- The quality of health & medical care is best if professional groups like physicians, nurses, paramedical workers, health educators, health visitors, public health engineers & many others share a common unifying goal.

- Teamwork can be defined as a dynamic process involving two or more two or more health care professionals with complementary background & skills, sharing common health goals & exercising concerted physical & mental effort in assessing, planning or evaluating patient care in health.
- care.

Functional classification of teams

Health care team:

It consists of all those who are involved in improving a community health setting without necessarily being in contact with patients actively.

Medical care team:

It consists of professionals & paraprofessionals that provide services for community health provide services for patients, generally in a hospital setting, without any direct or personal contact with them.

Patient care team:

It comprises any group of professionals & semiprofessionals in a hospital setting who jointly provide services that bring them in direct contact with patients.

Advantages of teamwork

- It gives a better end result with high-quality performance from each team member.
- It involve every person & his expertise & responsibilities.
- The execution of new ideas can be more effective & efficient through teamwork.
- It increase ownership with wider communication.
- It leads to information sharing & increases learning in the team & the organization.
- It provide more security & develops personal relationships.
- A particular problem can easily solved in team.
- It helps provide a variety of solutions.
- It increases the willingness of every member to take more risk.
- A team can handle more difficult & complex problem in the workplace.
- A team increases the accuracy of problem solving
- **Disadvantages of teamwork**
- It may lead to unequal participation of members in a team.
- Some individuals may be good workers,they may not be good team payers.
- It may limit creative thinking
- A team can sometimes take longer to produce desire results.
- Team can also result in added expenses
- It may face some inherent conflict
- Peer pressure
- Team can also result in added expenses
- It may face some inherent conflict
- Peer pressure

IV
Guidance & counseling

Meaning of Guidance:

Literally guidance means _to direct', _to point out', to show the path'. It is the assistance or help rendered by a more experienced person to a less experiences person to solve certain major problems of the individual (less experienced) i.e. educational, vocational, personal etc.

Concept of Guidance

is a concept as well as a process. As a concept guidance is concerned with the optimal development of the individual. As a process guidance helps the individual in self understanding (understanding one's strengths, limitations, and other resources) and in self-direction (ability to solve problems, make choices and decision on one's own).

Principles of Guidance:

Guidance is based upon the following principles.

i. **Holistic development of individual** : Guidance needs to be provided in the context of total development of personality.

ii. **Recognition of individual differences and dignity:** Each individual is different from every other individual. Each individual is the combination of characteristics which provides uniqueness to each person. Similarly human beings have an immense potential. The dignity of the individual is supreme.

iii. **Acceptance of individual needs:** Guidance is based upon individual needs i.e. freedom, respect, dignity.

iv. The individual needs a continuous guidance process from early childhood throughout adulthood.

v. Guidance involves using skills to communicate love, regard, respect for others.

Need And Importance of Guidance

Guidance is needed wherever there are problems. The need and importance of guidance are as follows.

- Self understanding and self direction: Guidance helps in understanding one's strength, limitations and other resources. Guidance helps individual to develop ability to solve problems and take decisions.
- Optimum development of individual
- Solving different problem of the individual
- Academic growth and development
- Vocational maturity, vocational choices and vocational adjustments
- Social personal adjustment
- Better family life
- Good citizenship
- For conservation and proper utilization of human resources
- For national development

Scope of Guidance

The fundamental aim of guidance programme being the maximum development of the child, all guidance programme must be geared toward attainment of the goal. Guidance services can assist the pupils in knowing themselves-their potentialities and limitations, making appropriate choices in educational, vocational and other fields. Some of the important guidance services are;

- The orientation services
- Student inventory services
- Career Information services
- Counseling services
- Group guidance services
- Placement services
- Research and evaluation services

Counseling

Definition and Meaning of Counselling

Counselling has been understood and defined in a number of ways.

According to Cormier and Hackney (1987) counselling is defined as the "helping relationship that includes –
a) someone seeking help,
b) someone willing to give help who is capable or trained to help,
c) a setting that permits help to be given and received.
Arbunckle has mentioned three points about counselling. They are:
a) Counselling is a process between two persons.
b) The basic aim of counselling is to help the person in solving his problems Independently.
c) Counselling is a professional job involving professionally trained persons. The following points below will give a clear picture as to what counselling is not.

What counselling is not:

- Counselling is not giving information alone, though information may be present
- Counselling is not giving advice
- Counselling is not influencing the clients' values, attitudes, beliefs, interests or decisions with or without any scolding, or compelling without the use of physical force
- Counselling is not interviewing, though interviewing is involved.

Therefore, the main objective of counselling is to bring about a voluntary change in the client.

Counselling can be of two types, individual or group. Individual counselling is done face to face and Group counselling is done to a group of individuals. Group counselling is a useful way of helping adolescents for addressing issues that are related to peer group influence.

Who can benefit from Counselling ?

All of us irrespective of our age, sex and profession have been taking help fromour elders, teachers and friends in solving certain problems.

Definition

According to Pepinsky & Pepinsky "counseling is an interaction which occurs between two individuals called counsellor and client which takes place in professional setting and is initiated to facilitate changes in the behaviour of a client".

Elements of counseling:

The key elements are:

- Building rapport and understanding
- Gathering data
- Finding out the problem
- Establishing personal involvement
- Giving hope
- Giving homework
- Terminating the counselling Elements are the first thing to be learned in any subject.

- Rapport
- Communication
- Counsellor's experience
- Counsellor's change to positive feelings
- Structured counselling interview

PRINCIPLES OF COUNSELLING

- Acceptance
- Individualization
- Privacy
- Confidentiality
- Accepting limitations
- Recording

Other Principles of Counselling

Counselling is based on n number of principles. These principles are: .

- Counselling is a process. It is necessary for the counsellor to understand that counselling is a process and a slow process. Failure to understand this will result in annoyance and disappointment.
- Counselling is for all. Especially in the school/college situation counselling is meant for all the students and not only for those who art: facing problems or other exceptional I students. As we have already discussed in the school situation counselling is more
- Counselling is based on certain fundamental assumptions. a) Every individual in this world is capable of taking responsibilities for him/her. b) Every individual has a right to choose his/her own path, based on the principles of democracy.
- Counsellor does not deprive the right of self-choice but simply facilitates choice. That counsellor should give due respect to the individual and accept him/her as he/she is.
- Counselling is not advice giving.
- Counselling is not thinking for the client, but thinking with the client. Counselling is for enabling the client to do judicious thinking.
- Counselling is not problem- solving. The counsellor simply assists the person to find solution on his/her own.
- Counselling is not interviewing but conversing with the client in order to help Him/her developing self understanding,
- The counsellor should determine individual differences and provide for them.
- The counsellor has to prepare the client to open to criticism including selfcriticism.
- The counsellor acts as a facilitator or catalyst only. He creates an atmosphere which is permissive and non -threatening, through his war111 and accepting relationship with the client which helps the client to explore himself/herself and understand himself/herself better.

Characteristics of Counselling

- Counselling is a profession dealing with Human Behaviour.
- It has its own standards of education and training which is formal.
- It has a systematic body of knowledge that can be imparted.
- It has a set of Technical Skills which may be acquired
- It is a learning oriented process.
- It is a face to face relationship.
- It is a democratic process.
- Successful counselling is based on Goal Setting and Attainment.
- It is based on Mutual and Professional Relationship.
- It takes place in a professional setting.

Types of Counselling

There is a number of counselling which take place these days. They are mainly divided as per the various fields. This allows people to choose the counsellor as per their specific problem. Moreover, this assures the counsellor doing the work is a specialist in their respective field. The following are the most common types of counselling:

- Marriage and Family Counselling
- Educational Counselling
- Rehabilitation Counselling
- Mental Health Counselling
- Substance Abuse Counselling

1. Marriage and Family Counselling

People often face a lot of problems in their marriage and family life. Sometimes, these troubled people find it hard to cope up with their life. This results in constant fights with their partners or family members. Marriage and family counselling comes in here. In other words, it helps people with these problems. They take them into confidence and prescribe solutions that will help them overcome their problems.

1. Educational Counselling

A student who is fresh out of school or college is often clueless as to which career to choose. This is completely normal for kids of that age to feel like that. Furthermore, sometimes even working individuals feel like that in the midst of their careers. This is nothing to worry about. Educational counselling helps these people in choosing their career path. They conduct seminars and orientations or private sessions where they discuss the interest of their client and offer solutions accordingly.

3. Rehabilitation Counselling

This type of counselling refers to a practice where the counsellor helps people with their emotional and physical disabilities. Furthermore, these counsellors teach these people ways to live independently and maintain gainful employment. It evaluates the strength and limitations of their patients. In short, they help people in guiding them and assisting them to lead independent lives.

4. Mental Health Counselling

Mental illnesses have become very common these days. Awareness has helped people identify the symptoms of it and visit mental health counsellors. Mental health counselling helps people deal with issues that impact their mental health and well-being. Some of the mental illnesses are depression, PTSD, ADHD, Bipolar disorder, and more. This counselling focuses on these issues and helps in resolving them for a healthier life.

5. Substance Abuse Counselling

Substance abuse counselling is a form of counselling which helps people in treating them and supporting them from breaking free from their drug and alcohol addiction. It helps people discuss the cause of this addiction and reach to the root of it. The counsellor thereby suggests coping strategies which make a positive impact on their lives. Moreover, they also provide them with practicing skills and behaviors which helps in their recovery.

In conclusion, all types of counselling carry equal importance. They allow people to work through their problems and lead a happier and healthier life. There is no shame in taking counselling sessions as it only helps in the growth of an individual. In addition, counselling also helps save lives.

Goals of Counselling

Goal is something that has to be achieved. Mainly there are three types of goals,

1. Immediate goal
2. Long term goal
3. Ultimate Goal

1.Immediate goal

Immediate goal means when a person comes to a counsellor our immediate goal is to give relief to the client; it can be given through supportive therapy or through the creation of rapport.

2. Long term goal

This is to make a client to a fully functioning person. These two goals can be achieved through a process or mediate goal. Precipitating factors and pre disposing factors are 12 Important when achieving goals. This process is achieved through self exploration that leads to behavioural change.

3. Ultimate goal

This is to make the client a fully functioning and to lead a good family life, to lead a creative life. Counselling has six major goals and they are:

- Achieving positive mental health
- Resolution of problem
- Improving personal effectiveness
- Modification of behaviour
- Helping to change
- Decision making

Many consider counselling a panacea for all ills, which is not true. Individuals have wide ranging ant1 many a time unrealistic expectations regarding counselling. This in turn led to disappointment. The reason for this state of affairs is lack 0f proper understanding as to what exactly are the goals of counselling. Some of the major goals of counselling generally accepted by counsellor are given below:

- Achievement of positive mental health Counselling An individual is said to have positive mental health when he is able to relate meaningfully with others and lead a fulfilling life. He is able to love and be loved. One goal of counselling is to help the individual to attain this state.
- Problem resolution Another goal of counselling is to help the individual to come out of a difficult situation or problem. It must be remembered that the individual is only assisted and he himself find solution for the problems.

- Counselling for decision-making Ability to make right and timely decisions is crucial for success in life. One major goal of counselling is to make individual capable of making independent decisions. Counsellor may 13 assist the individual by providing necessary informing or clarifying the counselee's goals, etc. but the decision should be taken by the counselee herself/herself.
- Improving personal effectiveness As effective person is one who is able to control impulses, think in creative ways and has the competence to recognize, define and solve problems. It can be seen that these different goals are not exclusive. These are all interdependent and overlapping.
- Help change For development, change is always necessary. Counselling helps individual to make changes in their attitude, perceptions or personality.
- Behaviour modification Another aim of counselling is to help in modifying behaviour. Removal of undesirable behaviour or self-defecting behaviour and learning desirable behaviour is considered necessary for attaining effectiveness and good adjustment. The behaviourally oriented counsellors are the chief proponents of this view.

Foundations of Counselling

There are main 3 foundations based on which Counselling is done:

- Philosophical Foundation
- Sociological Foundation
- Psychological Foundation.

Foundation of counselling includes many disciplines such as Philosophy, Sociology, and Psychology etc. Psychiatry, family studies and social work are the other disciplines that pave the foundations to counselling.

1.Philosophical foundation:

The philosophy deals with human values and the counselling gives importance to human value. The philosophy tells about the sense of purpose in life, while 17 counselling helps to attain or make him understand about the purpose of life. Philosophy tells about values, sensible, being considerable, being right and wrong etc. On the other hand, all these are practiced in counselling. Counselling beliefs in m,an's faith, his abilities and this is what philosophy teach us Smith's Philosophical Foundation of Counselling: o Faith in humanity o Concern for other person o Belief in potentiality and inner strength of man o Self responsibility o Freedom to choose sovergnity o Cherishing values of life.

2. Sociological foundation

It studies about how a man functions in social settings. In counselling, we deal with individual and their problem. Unless, we know about the society, we cannot solve the problem. Thus, the counsellor should know the culture and values of the society in which he is practicing counselling. Values, beliefs, systems acquired from the society can be useful in providing counselling. Counselling respects values, beliefs, systems of the client. Sociology teaches about the uniqueness about all these aspects. It also teaches about the various aspects of life. Each culture and system is different from the other; hence what is right in one culture may be wrong in another culture. Hence counselling must be based on the values of the client and not of the counsellor. Eg: Children sleeping with parents is accepted in India. But in the west it is not accepted.

3. Psychological foundation

Counselling deals with human behaviour and psychology is the scientific study of human behaviour. Counselling has roots in psychoanalysis (ego stages, free association, dream analysis). Functionalism in 1990's is an important aspect in counselling. Psychology also talks about the primary interest of the client. It deals with Motivation, Personality, Development stages, Memory, Nature and Nurture, defence Mechanism etc. It also talks about code of ethics which is applied in counselling. Concept of self and goal directed behaviour is very important in counseling.

Skills Needed In Counselling

Several skills need to be brought into a one-to-one counselling session. These include:

- Attitudinal skills;
- Listening skills;
- Verbal communication skills; and
- Giving leads.

Enlist the Counselling Skills

- Attending
- Observing
- Active listening
- Reflecting
- Questioning
- Summarizing
- Silence
- Independence
- Concreting
- Empathy and acceptance
- Cultural sensitivity

Counselling Process

When a person seeks counselling, he or she suffers from something serious be it mental issues, emotional problems, or family problems. The process isn't rushed but rather involves a systematic evaluation that includes a detailed process. The counselling process involves a step-by-step approach and the counselor conducts it in a way to make sure that his client is comfortable with the process. Lets have a look at the five crucial stages of a counselling process.

Steps of counseling

1: Building a Warm Relationship

When you are hitting up a counselor to discuss your problems, you ought to suffer from any serious issue concerning academics, relationships, career, or anything else. The first thing your expert does is to make yourself comfortable around him/her. He focuses on developing a warm relation and mutual trust first to make sure you do not hesitate while speaking about the problems you are facing.

2: Analysis

Now comes the second part, which is assessment. In this stage, the professional encourages you to speak in detail about your problems to grab the roots of the problem. He observes every minute detail from how you are speaking to your reactions to certain questions that might come from his end. Once he assesses the problem, the goal is fixed.

3: Setting the Goal

After a thorough evaluation of your problems, now comes the significant section of goal setting. Considering the issues you are facing the counselor sets a goal. That can be either you overcoming the problem or reconciling with it.

4: Plan of Action

The counselor plans an action for you to practice to see the results. Suppose someone has public speaking fear, The expert might ask him to practice speaking in front of the mirror. This is just an instance. Once you go through the plan for the desired tenure, he assesses your improvement. If things seem normal, you are at the final stage! If not, he might design something different.

BASIS FOR COMPARISON

GUIDANCE

COUNSELING

Meaning

Guidance refers to an advice or a relevant piece of information provided by a superior, to resolve a problem or overcome from difficulty.

Counseling refers to a professional advice given by a counselor to an individual to help him in overcoming from personal or psychological problems.

Nature

Preventive

Remedial and Curative

Approach

Comprehensive and Extroverted

In-depth and Introverted

What it does?

It assists the person in choosing the best alternative.

It tends to change the perspective, to help him get the solution by himself or herself.

Deals with

Education and career related issues.

Personal and socio-psychoological issues.

Provided by

Any person superior or expert

A person who possesses high level of skill and professional training.

Privacy

Open and less private.

Confidential

Mode

One to one or one to many

One to one

Decision making

By guide.

By the client.

5: Overcoming the Problem

As I mentioned in the previous point after you follow the plan of action the consequent results are taken into consideration. If things seem to go in the right direction and you start feeling relaxed, yes! You have achieved your goal.

Counselling Skills

Being a professional counselor requires some core skills to be able to handle client queries and drive the best results for them. The vital skills that a professional counselor must have are as follows:

Effective Listening:

A counselor must be a patient listener who not only listens to the clients queries but can handle them intricately. Without hearing the issues minutely, it is impossible to get ahead with the next counselling steps. Therefore, the counselor has to be someone with good listening skills who gives full attention to the client and their details.

A Good Communicator:

A counselor is someone who listens to his clients, analyses the problems, and develops a plan of action to achieve a target. It is indeed critical to be a very good communicator to help the person feel comfortable around him and make sure the client is not hesitating while speaking in front of him about his problems. Developing a good relationship is very important.

Analysis:

A successful counselor is someone who is not only a good listener but a good analyzer too, who uses his skills and expertise to reach the root of the problem and analyze it. Without analysis, the entire process is in vain as no goals can be set and the client will not be able to undergo any plan of action.

Comparison of guidance and councelling

Counselor

A counsellor is a person who is involved in counselling it refers to a person who is concerned with the profession of giving advice on various things such as academic smatters, vocational issues and personal relationship. He is generally a professional & an expert in his field of functioning. There are different types of counsellors

- Rehabilitation counselor
- Marriage and family counselor
- School counselor
- Mental health counselor
- Online counselor
- Legal counselor

Attitude of A Counsellor Positive Regard

Attributes of a Counsellor In order to provide effective counselling services, the counsellor needs to demonstrate certain attributes. Some of these attributes which makes a person a good counsellor are as under:

i. **Self-Awareness and Understanding:** A person who has awareness of her needs, motivation for helping, feelings, personal strengths and weakness acts as a good counsellor. These people do not use projection (for example: "I had a very aggressive counselee" instead of "I felt angry with the counselee"), defensiveness (for example: instead of responding to the counselee's feelings to a question" whether counselling will do any good", she may express her personal feeling to insecurity by raising her voice or other non-verbal behaviour.

ii. **Good Mental Health:** Although no person is totally problem free but a person with less problems of good mental health can be a good cousellor, otherwise their own problems will jeopardize the a process of counselling.

iii. **Sensitivity:** A person who is aware of resources, limitations, and vulnerability of other persons as well as is keenly perceptive to other persons feelings and needs are considered to have sensitivity. A person having the understanding of individual will act as a good counsellor. (A person who can put one's foot into other's shoe).

iv. **Open-Mindedness:** A person who is free from fixed or pre-conceived ideas. It does not mean that they have no personal values or beliefs, but they are aware of their own values and beliefs and are able to distinguish them from the beliefs and values of others. They do not thrust their values on others.

v. **Objectivity:** A person with the ability of not getting involved with the other person and at the same time, stand back and see accurately what is happening. (Not to get drowned while saving others.)

vi. **Approachability:** A person who has some resemblance with other known pleasant and friendly person, who is friendly, has positive attitudes about others and can be approached without a feeling of apprehension.

vii. **RESPECT** Whilst maintain a professional focus a counsellor able to show a genuine openness within the counselling relationship. A client must feel comfortable, safe and confident that 32 confidentiality will be maintained at all times and also that the counsellor is committed to helping and supporting.

viii. **EMPATHY** Empathetic understanding and ability to see things from the client's perspective is also important, as is the counsellors ability to demonstrate an investments of their time and full attention.

ix. **WARMTH AND UNDERSTANDING** Empathy and genuineness encourages clients to relax and trust. It also encourages client self disclosure. Maintaining warmth and understanding, without being judgemental, proves the client with a comfortable foundation relationship.

x. Counsellors also show their own personality and ensure there is a friendly atmosphere and attitude. In order to grow counselling relationship Conveying warmth through body language, using postures, maintaining eye contact and personal space, encouraging a client to trust the counsellor.

xi. Counsellors should also be aware of the way they speak-the tone of voice, speed of speech and delivery -as the word used should be in agreement with the way their body language provides reassurance. Warmth should be handled with care however, as a client who exhibits feeling of unease, distance and mistrust may feel initially threatened by sympathetic behaviour.

xii. A capable counsellor must possess a number of personal qualities and develop the proper attitudes to make a client feel at ease and to build rapport so that a client can self-disclose.

xiii. A counsellor should be agreeable and act appropriately to provide the client with a comfortable foundation for the counselling relationship.

Main Characteristics of A Good Counsellor

- A genuine interest in and respect for people from all walks of life.
- Patients understanding and the ability to listen non-judge mentally.
- Excellent oral and written communication skills and presentation skills.
- Objectivity and fact.
- The ability to motivate and inspire clients.
- The ability to facilitate communication in group of 8 to 20 people.
- Good organizational and planning skills.
- The ability to work effectively with others professional and community agencies.
- Help people to develop a better appreciation of their unique characteristics and how those characteristics relate to career choice.
- Help client's identity educational requirements and develop planning plans.
- Facilitate career management and career decision making workshop.
- Help the client deal with barriers to achieving their career plans.
- Provide current labor market information to help client make realistic occupational or employment decisions.
- Market clients to potential employers and help client to find job or work experience placement.
- Perform related administrative tasks such as keeping records.
- Plan and implement career and employment related programs
- Refer clients to appropriate service to address their particular needs.

Counseling is a process that enables a person to sort out issues and reach decision affecting their life. Often counseling is sort out of times of chances of crisis, it needs not to be so, however, as counseling can also help us at any time of our life.

Difference Between Councelling And Health Education
Councelling
Health Education

- Counselling is a two-way interaction between a client and a provider. It is an interpersonal, dynamic communication process that involves a kind of contractual agreement between a client and a counsellor who is trained to an acceptable standard and who is bound by a code of ethics and practice. It requires empathy, genuineness and the absence of any moral or personal judgement.
- Counselling can be applied to any life situation, for example, when a nurse is listening and talking to grieving relatives; or a colleague is talking to someone who wants to quit their job and even commit suicide because of it! In other words, counselling is not peculiar only to STIs and HIV.

- Counselling aims to encourage healthy living and requires the client to explore important personal issues and to identify ways of living with the prevailing situation, whether it is an infection or bereavement. It is not about providing advice or guidance, nor does it mean befriending someone.

- Health education is the provision of accurate and truthful information so that a person can become knowledgeable about the subject and make an informed choice.

Role of a nurse in counseling

Using the therapeutic relationship, the nurse performs the role of counsellor to help people focus on a goal or outcome and develop strategies that support self-care and enable individuals and their families to take responsibility for and participate in decisions about their health.

- He/she can provide a range of services including education, research and knowledge sharing, evidence informed practices; system navigation and communication.
- Nurses can provide an opportunity for people to work towards living in a more satisfying and resourceful way and use a range of counseling skills.
- Nurse can assist the people to be supported, to gain insight and to bring about change in thoughts, feelings and behavior.
- Nurse can provide intake coordination, assessment, treatment (including counseling, group therapies) and follow-up care for children, youth, adults, seniors and their families with addictions, mental illness and mental problems using common

Assessment tools.

- Nurses does supervision/monitoring of medication and application of psychosocial skills. With ongoing evaluation of outcomes, nurses can make appropriate referrals depending on the identified needs of the person and address issues of stigma associated with having mental illness.

Crisis Counseling:

- Establish rapport
- Tell their story
- Identify major problem(s)
- Assess for safety issues
- Deal with feelings
- Explore alternatives

- Develop action plan
- If appropriate, make referrals (ongoing services or crisis services).

Crisis Counseling:

Safety:

Ensures the individual is safe. If lethality existed before crisis counseling, this risk has been reduced and resources, if available, have been provided

Stability:

Ensures the individual is stable and has a short-term plan which includes mastery of self and the emergency or disaster situation

Connection:

Helps connect the individual to formal and informal resources and support. If resources are supports are not readily available, crisis counseling helps the individual pursue potential natural supports/resources.

V

Principal of Education and teaching learning process

Introduction

Education is the corner stone of Nursing profession. Education in Health care has both the patient education and Nursing staff student education. It is a topic of utmost interest to nurses in every setting in which they practice. Teaching is a major aspect of Professional role. Nursing has been called "the oldest of the art and youngest of the professions" (Donabue, 1985). Planning for nursing Education may form the Education for the other health and development professionals who also take into account the characteristics of society as a whole. Nursing Education is the "Production aspect" of Nursing manpower development.

Nursing Education is also coordinated with the Education of the professionals in allied sectors of Health and Development. Education encompasses both the teaching and learning of knowledge, proper conduct and technical competency. It thus focuses on the cultivation of skills,trades or professions as well as mental, moral and aesthetic development.

It aims the harmonious development of the physical, intellectual, social, emotional, spiritual and aesthetic powers or abilities of the student in order to render professional nursing care to people of all ages, in all phases of health and illness, in a variety of settings, in the best or highest possible manner.

Definitions

Education is the all-round drawing out of the best in child and man- body, mind and spirit"

– Mahatma Gandhi.

"Education is the natural, harmonious and progressive development of man's innate powers".

– Pestalozzi.

Nursing Education

Nursing education is a professional education which is consciously and systematically planned and implemented through instruction and discipline.

Principles of nursing education

- **Caring:** In order to care for others, onemust first care for self.
- **Integrity:** Integrity encompasses theability to communicate honestly and sincerely, and take responsibility for one's actions.
- **Diversity:** Diversity does more thanacknowledge and advocate for differences of backgrounds and experiences.
- **Excellence:** Excellence is achieved throughengagement in scholarship, professional growth, and continual improvement.
- **Other principles**

Encourage contact between students and faculty.

- Develop reciprocity and cooperation among students.

  - Encourage active learning.
  - Give prompt feedback
  - Emphasize time on task.
  - Communicate high expectations

Respect diverse talents and ways of learning

Philosophy of nursing education

- Beliefs and values with regard to man in general and specifically man as the learner, teacher, nurse and the client and the beliefs about health, illness, society, nursing, and learning etc.
- Seeks to study the process and discipline of education in order to understand how it works, improve its methods and perfect its applications in society.
- To improve education and its systems and methods for the betterment of humanity.
- Ideally, it informs and raises the quality of curriculum, teaching methods and the overall educational experience.

Definitions

Philosophy

Philosophy is a search for a comprehensive view of nature, an attempt at a universal explanation of nature of things

– Henderson.

Philosophy is the science of knowledge.

– Fitche

Philosophy is the science of all sciences.

– Coleridge

Philosophy is the mother of all arts and the true medicine of the mind.

– Cicero.

"Philosophy of nursing education is the written statement of the believes, values, attitudes and ideas which the faculty as a group agreed upon in relation to the nursing educational program such as health, disease, nursing, nurse, nursing profession, education, learner, society, patient nursing education and preparation of nurses."

1. **Relationship between Philosophy and Education, 2.Types of Philosophy**

    3. Traditional Philosophy

- **Naturalism**

    - It is concerned with nature and believes that reality and nature are identical and beyond nature there is no reality.
    - For naturalist, nature is everything and nothing exists superior than nature so they separates nature from God. Man is regarded as a child of nature.
    - Naturalists also believe that all our activities, whether it may be biological, psychological or social are initiated by our instincts.
    - Natualism stresses the need to return to the nature from artificiality.

- **Idealism**

    - Idealism is the oldest philosophy. It believes that man is the combination of spiritual and material aspects, the spiritual aspect is more real and important.
    - Idealism regards spirit and intellect are of supreme value than physical matter. As per the idealism individual experience is valid than the material world and man lives in the world of ideas rather than facts.

- **Pragmatism**

    - Pragmatism means thinking of or dealing with problems in a practical way rather than by using theory or abstract principles.

- ○ Pragmatism is essentially a humanistic philosophy maintianing that man creates his won values in course of activity, that reality is still making and awaits its part of completion from the future.

- **Realism**

  - ○ According to this, things we see and perceive are real and knowledge acquired through senses is true.
  - •

"Realism is the reinforcement of our common acceptance of this world as apears to us"
– Butter

1. **Modern contemporary philosophy**

Existentialism
It is the youngest philosophy, described as modern 20 th century philosophy.
Meaning:
This philosophy stresses theimportant of human experience and says that everyone is responsible for the results of their own action.
Assumptions
The center of existence is man rather than truth, laws, principles or essence.
Man is not alone in the world. Man is a social being.
Man cannot accept the ready-made concepts of existence forced upon him
Man is free agent capable of shaping his own live and shaping his own destiny.Man is not complete: Man has to meet the challenges in the changing society.
Progressivism
It is an American philosophy.
Meaning
Progressivism is the theory of education that is concerned with learning by doing that children learn best when pursuing their own interest and satisfying their needs.
Behaviourism
Person's behavior is the result of environmental conditioning. Man is a passive recipient, who reacts to external stimuli, he has no will or decision of his own or the capacity to take spontaneous action.
Principles
Individual's action are predetermined by his heredity or immediate surroundings.
Man is not separate from his surrounding environment.
Human behavior is controlled by creativity.
Educational applications

- Learning is governed by man's action and reaction to various media (oral, written,machine).
- Learning occurs as a personal achievement through interaction between the learner and environment.

Humanism
Man is an end, not a means.
Principles
The humanist emphasis is on literature. He has to overcome the conflicts of his own time.
The role of Education

- Children must be taught to respect language, a sense of language perfection.

- Children must be trained in modern literary standards of academics

Experimentalism

It believes that things are constantly changing. It is based on the view that reality is what works right now. Schools exist to discover and expand the society we live in. Students study social experiences and solve problems

Man is a social being and product of his environment. Learning depends on experiment.

Eclecticism

It is the process of pulling out and putting together of the useful and essential aspects of various philosophies of education.

Meaning

- The fusion or synthesis of different philosophies of education.
- The process of putting together the common views of different philosophies into comprehensive whole.

Aims of education

Education is a continuous lifelong process. The aim of education is to provide direction to the process of education. There are different aims of education like social aim, vocational aim, cultural aim, moral aim, spiritual aim, intellectual aim, etc.

- **Social Aim**

  Human being is considered to be a social animal. Education can make him to be a productive member of the society. Every individual is born with some potential. It is the education that helps the individual to meet his potential. Society is considered to be the result of interaction among the individuals either in small or large group. Education ensures peaceful existence of the society. By education, students realize the importance of social values like justice, fair play, healthy competition and harmony, etc. Education makes the individual accountable to the community and the nation. With social aims, education gives direction to the society in its development.

- **Vocational Aim**

  Process of education makes the individual to be capable of his livelihood, so that he can useful and lead a productive life in the society. The individual respects the dignity of labour. This aim makes him self-reliant and sufficient and fills the gap between education and vocation. Vocational aim has utilitarian dimension too. Education provides knowledge and skills to an individual in a fruitful manner.

- **Cultural Aim**

  Education has a cultural aim also. By undergoing education, child becomes civilized and cultured. An educated person develops aesthetic sense and respects other's culture. Knowing the culture includes gaining or acquiring knowledge about existing beliefs of a society, art, morals, laws, etc.

- **Moral Aim**

  Education helps in building up of character of an individual. Most values like honesty, truthfulness, justice, goodness, purity, courage, punctuality, and dutifulness are nurtured through education.

- **Spiritual Aim**

  Education is necessary to promote spirituality among the individuals. He raises himself above self-interest and works for the welfare of others, which is called to be the state of self-actualization. He not only preaches right or wrong, but also practices it in his life.

- **Intellectual Aim**

  Education provides opportunities to an individual to develop innate power or intellectual capacity to think rationally and lead his life independently with confidence

- The child should become efficient member of society.

- Promotion of good health
- Skillful training.
- Development of moral character.

Function of Education
Education has a number of functions towards the child as an individual, society, and nation.
Towards the Individual

1. Education promotes the growth and development of an individual. Education provides growth in whole personality of the child through formal training.
2. Education provides direction and guidance to the individual. It is helpful to channelize the energy of the child to more productive activities.
3. Education prepares the child for adult life, so that he can take up responsibilities as an adult.
4. Education is helpful in conservation of old traditions, values, ideas, customs, etc.
5. Education is the means of transmitting culture from one generation to another.
6. Education provides new experiences, unfolds new dimensions of knowledge, and furthers civilization and culture.
7. Education prepares the individual for a vocation, by helping him acquire knowledge and skills.
8. Vocational preparation helps in achieving self-reliance and sufficiency.
9. Educational aims at all round development of the individual, so promotes holistic personality development.
10. Education is essential for moral and character development.
11. Education helps in creating awareness about the past and the present and prepares the individual for the future.
12. Education helps the individual in maintain his livelihood.

Towards the society

1. Education promotes the holistic development of individuals, who are the members of the society. This ultimately ensures growth of society in the right direction.
2. Education prepares good citizens in a civilized society, who can enjoy full privileges, freedom, exercise their rights, and at the same time fulfill the responsibilities towards the society and the nation.
3. Education is essential for ensuring civilization and cultural security. With the individual sense of civilization and presentation of traditional culture, civilization and culture security is promoted.

Towards the Nation

1. Education is required for the development of a nation. Education promotes literacy and the availability of the resources.
2. Education is required to maintain the national integrity. Education widens the thinking of an individual and he can work for the national integration. He can fight against casteism, communalism, regionalism, etc., that act as barrier to the national integrity.
3. Education prepares the task force, who can provide their services for the smooth functioning of a nation.
4. Education helps in building up the leaders required for the social, economic, and political growth of a country. The prepared leaders can meet the country's immediate and future needs and promote stable society required for the growth of a nation.

Teaching
Definitions
Different authors have tied to define teaching from their own point of view. Some of the definitions in chronological order are given as under:

H.C. Momson (1 934): Teaching is an intimate contact between a more mature personality and less mature one which is designed to fixther the education of the latter.

John Brubacher (1 939): Teaching is an arrangement and manipulation of a situation in which there are gaps and obstructions which an individual will seek to overcome and from which he will learn in course of doing so.

a American Educational Research Association Commission in "Handbook of Research on Teachingw (1 962): Teaching is a f6rm of interpersonal influence aimed at changing the behaviour potential of another person.

B.O. Smith (1963): Teaching is a system of actions involving an agent, an end in view and a situation i-ncluding two sets of factors - those over which the agent has no control (class size, size of class room, physical characteristics of pupils etc.) and those that he can modify (ways of asking questions, instructional methods and ways of structuring information or ideas etc.)

Burton (1 963): Teaching is the stimulation, guidance, direction, and encouragement of learning.

Israel Shefflar (1966): Explained teaching may be characterized as an activity aimed at an achievement of learning, and practiced in such a manner as to respect the student's intellectual integrity and capacity.

I Clark (1970): Teaching refers to activities that are designed and performed to produce change in student's (pupil) behaviour

Ned A. Flanders (1970) described: Teaching as an interaction process. Interaction means participation of both teacher and students and both are benefited by this. 'Ihe interntion takes place for achieving desired objectives.

Concepts These definitions reveal the following conceptual aspects of teaching:

i. Teaching is an interactive process, which takes place between teacher and students to influence each other.
ii. The interactive teaching activities are designed to promote desired change in students' behaviouf, i.e., to achieve desired objectives. In other words &achingis goaldirected
iii. Thcbing is based on students' intellectual level and capacity.
iv. Teaching takes place in a situation having controllable and incontrollable factors.
v. Teaching is the task of a teacher who not only imparts informations but also motivates, guides, helps and encourages students to learn.

Characteristics of teaching

In order to achieve significant success in education, students and teachers need to develop mutual trust. Of course, teachers have a great responsibility for creating a positive classroom atmosphere, because their task is to convey knowledge to students and prepare them for all the challenges that lie ahead. Many characteristics of teaching essential both for success in school and life arise from that relationship.

1. Active learning techniques

It has long been known that classes where the teacher talks incessantly throughout the lecture, while the students are passive listeners, do not yield satisfactory results. Modern education requires active student participation, which can be achieved by using some of the following active learning techniques:

- **Discussion** – classroom is a place where students are entitled to their own opinion regarding the topic that is being discussed. It is important that students have their own attitude, because that way, they will look at the lesson being covered from their own, personal angle. In addition, discussion yields answers to various questions that may not have been even asked otherwise.

1. **Brainstorming** – creative thinking and sharing ideas on a given topic is a great learning technique, because it encourages students to come up with a solution together. In brainstorming, there are no wrong answers, which relieves students of the anxiety that they have done something wrong.

- **Note taking** – active note taking means covering a lesson "in one's own words" (instead of merely copying what the teacher says). Another great example of active note taking is creating one's own system of explanations and linking terms with certain parts of the text. Notes created in this way improve student comprehension of the teaching material, and encourage them to always seek and write down answers to the questions that interest them.

- **Teamwork** – joint problem solving during lectures and work on school projects are highly effective teaching methods for student engagement. Instead of passively listening to the teacher's presentation, students help each other to achieve a common goal.

Applying what one has learned outside the classroom is another great method of active learning. There are various methods where children can reach answers to the questions asked in class through play. This way, they acquire necessary experience through practical examples, which is very important for the understanding of the lesson.

2. Great learning environment

Environment in which teaching takes place is extremely important for a positive learning experience. To make students feel comfortable, schools strive to create an inspirational learning environment. The classroom is a central place for educational activities, which is why it should be visually appealing. This is why classrooms are usually filled with colorful posters and pictures that send positive messages (respect your classmates, read books, eat healthy, etc.).

If the classroom is equipped with modern technologies, it will additionally facilitate both students' learning and teachers' instruction because computers and tablets provide a multimedia experience familiar and relatable to younger generations. A great learning environment also helps in overcoming psychological school-related challenges, such as the fear of the unknown, depression, shyness, etc. As a result of a positive approach, students respond better to lessons and consequently achieve better results in tests.

3. Clear communication

The way in which the teacher communicates with students is crucial for learning. Teachers' manner and approach to students may vary, while some are relaxed, others firmly believe in maintaining discipline. Regardless of the personal style, a good teacher is expected to present the lesson in a clear and age-appropriate way.

The subject areas are often extremely complex, e.g. computer science, but that does not mean that the lesson should be impossible to understand. Every information can be conveyed in an engaging and clear manner, especially if the information is linked to good examples from everyday life. Students should ask different questions during class, and the teacher should answer them clearly and precisely.

Clear communication is also important in class when student knowledge is tested during the school year (both orally and in writing). Test questions must be clearly formulated so as to avoid insecurity and confusion in students. The same applies to oral exams, where clear communication is even more important, for example, the teacher's criteria and the level of knowledge needed to get a passing or good grade. In this way, conflict and stressful situations which could ruin a positive classroom atmosphere are avoided.

4. Good relationship between teacher and student

Student-teacher relationships should be characterized by mutual respect. To build such a positive relationship, both sides have to demonstrate positive qualities. On the one hand, teachers will earn students' respect if they set clear and fair rules. Effective classroom management is very important in this case since students expect a certain level of discipline and the lack of it may cause an unproductive classroom atmosphere.

In addition to clearly presented rules of conduct, the teacher builds the relationship by proving his/her competency by demonstrating knowledge in class (answering student questions, designing creative lessons). Showing interest in students' needs and recognizing their personal talents will improve the level of trust which directly affects the quality of teaching.

As respect is a two-way street, students should also demonstrate willingness and be cooperative in class. Showing respect for the teacher's work is not only important for high-quality teaching with less stress, but also shows respect for authority, which is very important for one's future career where students will find themselves in different roles, and where their career may often depend on how they treat their coworkers.

5. Critical thinking

One of the main teaching goals is the development of critical thinking in students. It helps them to combine acquired knowledge, and personal skills and attitudes to correctly interpret the obtained information. In practice, this means that teachers should encourage students to interpret the received information in their own way, and to take a certain position which they will defend with arguments. This is one of the requirements for successfully overcoming obstacles in life, which is why critical-thinking education is extremely important both in modern education, and life in general.

Critical thinking is also important in education, because it helps one to see the world from a personal angle, thus developing positive qualities in children. This is why various techniques of critical thinking are implemented since elementary education, through high school, and finally in higher education. The higher the level of education, the more important critical thinking becomes because it helps students to obtain significant knowledge and scientific achievements.

Students will face various situations in their lives where they will need to assess the situation and make a decision based on the acquired knowledge and experience, instead of external pressure or propaganda.

6. Problem solving

One of the most important characteristics of teaching is problem solving. Not only is overcoming obstacles crucial for successful education, but it also represents the foundation for a successful professional and private life. Although it may not seem like it, teachers find it hard to define tasks that will be challenging enough without being too hard. Appropriate tasks will not make students feel helpless and inadequate, but will encourage them to work toward a solution.

Problem solving helps in the development of important qualities, such as patience, teamwork, diligence, and logical reasoning. In addition, by solving challenges through the application of the knowledge acquired in class, students begin to understand the practical value of learning. All this knowledge improves one's learning in school, but also understanding of everyday challenges.

Principles and Maxims of Good Teaching

Good teaching means effective and efficient teaching i.e. teaching is ac'cording to level of students and it helps students in achieving expected gain in knowledge, comprehension, competencies and attitudes. There are some general principles and maxims of teaching methods which must be followed by every teacher to conduct good teaching. These are as under:

a) General Principles

1) Principle of Setting Definite Goals and Objectives

The goals and objectives must be set according to the expected standards and outcomes in students, These should be clear to both, teachers and students. The goals and objectives should be definite and clearly stated to be able to plan, implement and evaluate teaching learning activities effectively.

2) Principle of Student Centeredness

The teaching is for the student's to achieve educational objectives, therefore it is very important that the teaching strategies planned by the teacher should be according to the level of students, their abilities, interests etc.

3) Principle of lndividhl Diflerence

All children are different with respect to their abilities, interests etc. The teacher needs to consider individual differences for her teaching to be effective.

4) Principle of Motivation

Motivation is stimulating interests. The teacher needs to do her best to create interest (motivate) among students in the teaching lessons. Once the interest is created in students, they will become attentive, comprehend and work better and thus learning is done. The motivation can be done by the following techniques.

i. Linking teaching- learning with life experiences, important happenings, with some examples.
ii. Satisfying curiosity of students. Answering queries, linking them with students' queries.
iii. Making use of natural urges and acquired interests e.g., the system of having class representative, class-room committees etc. This gives students opportunity to satisfy their ego, self assertion and learn to take

responsibilities. This in turn motivates students in their studies.

iv. Utilizing all the senses of children. The teacher needs to make use of variety of teaching aids as these stimulate and sustain interest of students in teaching lessons.

5) " Principle of Activity or Learning by Doing

Teaching is effective only when learners are active in the class-room and outside the class-room, both physically and mentally. When learners are active, learning becomes easier, quicker and more effective, therefore the teacher needs to plan teaching-learning activities where students can make direct observation to the situation, phenomena etc., participate in doing certain activities during the class and after the class, do certain mental exercises, solve problems, plan and organize certain social services etc. Thus, it stimulates interest and effective learning takes place.

6) Principle of Connecting with Life

The effective learning takes place when teaching is done in the social context and linked with the life experiences.

7) Principle of Active Involvement and Participation of Students

The students are no more passive listener to what is being taught by the teacher. They need to be actively involved in all the stages of teaching-learning process according to their level of readiness i.e. state of mind. This would not only provide input from the students but will make them aware of what is being planned and what is expected from them in the teaching-learning programme.

8) Principal of correlation

Knowledge is not fragmented. There exist links among various subjects, in the same subject, between the present and the past etc. Future can be predicted on the basis of present situations. The teacher therefore, needs to identify the linking ideas and events and correlate while teaching various lessons to make effective teaching.

9) The Principle of Feedback, Reinforcement and Remedial Teaching

The teacher needs to device feedback mechanisms to laow the results of teaching and accordingly give positive reinforcements in the form of praise, grades, certificates and other incentives. Some students may lag behind and need to have remedial teaching. The teacher may have to arrange extra coaching classes, additional assignments etc.

10) Principle of Creating Conducive Environment

It is very important to have suitable physical and social environment to motivate students to learn. The teacher should see that there is proper arrangement of classroom, its furniture, lighting etc., there is proper discipline and order in the students, the students are co-operative, help each other etc.

1I) Principle of Planning Teaching and its Effective Strategies

It is very important for the teacher to plan lesson content, teaching aids, teaching methods, teaching-learning activities and an outline of the plan to be implemented. This way the teaching becomes objective based. It helps in following all the principles of teaching. The learning is also more effective.

12) ' The Principle of Change and Rest

There should be appropriate provision of change, rest and recreation otherwise it leads to fatigue, boredom and lack of concentration. The time table should be well balanced. Two consecutive period of the same subjects should be avoided.

b) Maxims of Teaching

Maxims of teaching are the basic rules of teaching which when implemented motivate learners, promote their attention on what is being taught, encourage their active involvement and thus result in effective learning. The teacher needs to know them and practice. Brief description of the maxims is presented in this section.: Maxims of teaching

1) Proceed From Known to Unknown

The teaching is always done step by step. The new lesson should be related to what is already learnt i.e. what is known to them. The teacher can show the similarities and dissimilarities of the new lesson with the old lesson. This would not only create interest in students but also make the learning meaningful and lively. For example while teaching about the pathological changes in a particular organ of the body it can be started by review of its normal structure and functions.

2) Proceed from simple to complex

This maxim implies that the content of the lesson is organized in a manner that those ideas which art. elementary and easier to understand by the students are put up in the beginning and tril-thier details follow the proper order. For example teaching of anatomy and physiology of a pamūlar organ. It initiates with gross structure to minute structcre fi~llovvcd by its hnctiolis and role in the body.

3) Proceed from Indefinite to Definite

Nursing students who enter school/college of nursing, usually have vague ideas about human body, health and disease, about care of patients, their rehabilitation etc. The purpose of teaching in nursing is to make these ideas clear and precise so that students have definite picture in their mind and develop desired attitude and skills. It is therefore very importa~~t for the teacher to plan the lesson carefully, make use of variety of methods and Audio-visual aids, give live experiences etc. to clarify the ideas.

4) Proceed from Concrete to Abstract

This maxim implies that students would understand new ideas better when teacher makes use of clear and vivid illustrations,.examples, concrete objects, models, actual field visits etc. For example, anatomy of an organ can be learnt by handling the actual organ and by doing its dissection. Disposal of sewage can be best understood by visiting sewage disposal plant.

5) Proceed from Particular to the General

This maxim implies that before telling general rules or principles to the class, the teacher presents particular facts ancl exanlplcs. After study of these facts, the students themselves come out with general rules and principles. For exaniple the definition and underlying causes of head sores can be generalised by the students after consideration of particular facts and instances of bed sores. This principle is applied in the inductive method of teaching.

6) Proceed from Inductive to Deductive approach

It implies using of inductive method of teaching. In this method of tcaching the teacher begins with the presentation of facts, examples to the students. The students after consideration of facts and exa:cples and after close and correct obsei-mtions, establish general ruies/principles/definitions and uses etc. Closely associated to this approach, is the deductive approach. In this approach the teacher presents general rules/principles/definitions to the students. The students arc asked to apply it to particular examples. For esarnplc definition and general causes of lēti sores are presented to ihe students, thcy are then asked to ic!ent~fy cases of bed sores and specify the underlying causes. Both these methods go together and are irilportant for effective teaching as students becotne mentally active and get {notivated. These rnethods involve the process of analysis and synthesis.

Functions of a Teacher

- Creating and maintaining desirable learning environment.
- Motivating students to learn.
- Arranging for conditions which would provide opportunities to develop desired comprehension, competencies and attitudes.
- Utilizing the initiatives and natural urges of students to facilitate learning.
- Guiding and helping students to develop creative abilities.
- Guiding and helping students to develop inductive and deductive abilities.
- Diagnosing learning problems of students.
- Planning and implementing remedial measures.
- Evaluating records and reports
- Participating in planning and organizing of curriculum.

Qualities of a Good Teacher

A good teacher possesses the following qualities. A good teacher:

- Has mastery of the subject matter,

- Is skillful and artistic in teaching methods and in guiding learning,
- Treats each individual as unique and recognizes individual differences,
- Encourages self learning,
- Keeps the students active and disciplined,
- Is kind and sympathetic,
- Plans herhis teaching carefully in advance but is not very rigid with the plan,
- Is approachable and seeks the co-operation of the leal-t-ners.

Learning

Gates, Jersild and IvlcConnell highlighted: "Learning may be thought of as the progressive change in bchaviour which is associated, on the one hand, with successive presentations of a situation and on the other, with repeated efforts of the individual to react it effectively'".

According to Heidgerken: "Learning may be defined as the mental activity by ineans of which knowledge, skills, attitxdes, appreciations and ideals are acquired resulting in the modification of behaviour.

The modification comes through knowledge and experience: it involves no additions or substractions of knowledge and experiences as such, but rather implies something new which has not existed for that individual before.

- Learning is the addition of new knowledge in the light of past knowledge and experience". These definitions reveal the following concepts of learning :
- Learning is a process of modification and implies a progressive change in behaviour as a result of synthesis of old and new knowledge and experience.
- Learning is developing abilities to respond to various situations intelligently and meaningfully.
- Learning can be accomplished by learner's own active efforts,
- Learning is mental activity which involves the process of conceptualization, description, inductive and deductive reasoning for acquiring knowledge, attitudes and skills.

Characteristics of Learning

The primary characteristics of learning which have been presented by Heidgerken as applied in the teaching and the learning of nursing are briefly discussed in this section.

1.Learning is Unitary:

It implies that the learner reacts as a whole person to the wholesituation in a unified way. It means that the learner responds ' intellectually. emotionally, physically and spiritually at the same time. The response by the learner is to the entire learning situation rather than to ariy one stimulus and in a unified way. This coordinated and integrated total reaction of the leainer to the learning situation helps achieve educational goals. Each learner responds differently to teaching-learning situation because each lemer is different in all aspects. There are inany factors from within the individual and in the learning situation which interfere with or promote unified responses. It is very important for the teachers in nursing schools and colleges to understand the unitary characteristic of learning and put into practice.

2) Learning is Individual and Social:

The very fact that learning is a self active process, it emphasiēs that learning is an individual matter. Each individual has to do herlhis own learning. Each individual differ in this depending upon inherited traits, health, home training, social environment, educational opportunities, self determination etc. Learning is also social in 3 larger sense because it takes place in response to the environment in which there are other individuals, social groups and physical things. Individual's learning is influenced by her is parents and family members, friends, relatives, neighboras. class mates etc. and learn their ideas, notions. feelings, attihide etc. Social agencies like family, play grounds, youth clubs, templelchurch, school etc. play very important role in the learning process. The nursing teachers must consider variations among learners and should not Teaching-Learning in expect same quantity and degree of perfection in learning at the same time. Nursing Education Rather, these variations should be studied in each teaching-learning situation and accordingly handle the situation for effective learning.

3) Learning is Self-active:

This characteristic of learning implies that the learner can learn only through herhis own active response to teachinglearning situation, i.e., the individual has to undertake self leaming activities. Without self-activities there is no learning. The various self activities include listening attentively, visualizing attentively, making observation carefully,, reacting and acting tn situation, asking questions for clarification, taking down notes, search literature, do self study, recall, memorize, do analysis and return demonstration, practice etc. Students need to develop their own habits of learning. The teacher can simply help and guide them to develop proper habits and direct them to undertake suitable self-learning activities to achieve educational goals.

4) Learning is Purposive:

Learning is always based on purpose. No learning takes place without any purpose. Purpose gives directions and thus determines goals for leaming. The goals determined are based on students leaming needs as related to their desires, interests, attitudes etc. The teacher needs to set desirable goals by involving students and considering their needs, desires, interests etc.

5) Learning is Creative:

Learning is a process in which the potentialities within the individual are created in to actualities both by herhis own initiative and also by the assistance of others. In simple words it can be said that there are two dynamic factors in creative learning and these are: i) the natural responses of learner's mind i.e. internal force and ii) intellectual guidance from the. teacher. Both these factors are vital. But, it is the learner who decides and makes choices out of internal motivation as to what, how and when to do in response to the demands of existing situation. Thus learning results in new organization of knowledge and pattern of experiences which has not happened before. The leamer develops unique and distinctive pattern of behaviour and that is what the creative learning is.

6) Learning is Transferable:

This characteristic of learning implies that what is learnt in one context or situation will apply or affect another situation. True learning transfers but it depends upon understanding of principles, concepts, their relationships which have been generalised by the learner and applied deliberately to the solution of practical problems. The teacher should provide opportunities and should see that nursing students apply the principles which they have learnt in the class room while giving nursing care to the patient.

7) Learning Affects the Conduct of Learner:

Learning results in acquisition of knowledge, skills and brings in change in attitude. This modifies the conduct of learner

Factors Affecting Learning and Teaching

Learning does not take place in vacuum. By and large it goes along with teaching process. Both learning and teaching are always under the influence of certain factors within the learner, teacher and in the environment-both physical and social. These factors include:

- Intelligence of the learner Hereditary endowment
- Motivation
- Good physical health
- Maturation
- The study habits
- Emotional stability Prejudices, biases etc
- The learning experience
- The learning situation
- The teacher – his/her personality, activities, guidance and instructions
- Teaching techniques
- The school environment

- The presence or absence of some of these factors determines the effectiveness of learning and teaching.

VI
Methods of Teaching

To achieve the goal of teaching, the teacher must adopt effective teaching methods in education. The teacher has many options to choose from different teaching techniques designed specifically for teaching and learning. Writing lesson plans is a foremost thing that a teacher must do before executing any teaching strategy in the class.

The teaching method should be adopted on the basis of certain criteria like the knowledge of the students, the environment and the set of learning goals decided in the academic curriculum. Students respond differently to different methods of teaching.

LECTURE METHOD

The first method of teaching is known as lecture method. Lecture method is the type of method which involves formal of a discourse of a sum. It is an instruction technique which is presented orally. A teacher or lecture exemplifies a one communication term; it is used to introduce the course material to give students.

Advantages: The following are the advantages of lecture method

- The teacher is in total control of the classroom.
- It saves time to cover a wider topic.
- It makes a teacher an active participant.
- However the following are the disadvantages of lecture method. it is teacher centered
- learners becomes passive recipients it encourages one way communication slow learners may miss important points encourages learners to depend on the teacher
- Every method of teaching is applicable in many subjects.However lecture method is applicable in the informational subjects.
- Lecture method is one the methods which can be improve by the teacher and the students.
- The teacher should create lesson to be conducive by allowing students to take part in the lesson.

Demonstration Method

This method involves the presentation of a pre-arranged series of events to a group for their observation. This is accompanied by explanatory remarks. This method is most commonly used in science and fine arts. It can be used in giving information, training and knowledge. Anderson (1903:9), further contributed that, —the demonstrations should be selected both in terms of the needs of the observers as well as the ideas, materials, procedures or techniques which can be observed profitably.

Advantages Of Demonstration

- The demonstrations can open a student's eye to a new world of understanding.
- The demonstration shortens the time for learning and lengthens the memory of facts and principles.
- The demonstration is quite effective in making clear to the participants and observers the relationship between skills and their purpose.

- The demonstrations foster good thinking in group and individuals.
- The demonstration aids in bringing about a relationship between the theory and practice.
- Thus, demonstration, if it is well planned, conducted and followed, can be a useful approach in teaching.

Disadvantages

- It has no permanent record; one can be too slow or fast.
- It can be expensive in terms of material costs.
- It can be too long and in consequence, learners may lose interest.
- Teachers need a lot of time to rehearse.

To make this method improved and successful, a teacher must plan the demonstrations in great detail and rehearse it; make sure that all the material and illustrations are nearby when the demonstrations begins; and a teacher must break down the demonstration into a simple step-by-step pattern so that it can be easily understood by the class.

Sir John (1964:302) added that,

—to enhance this demonstration in a classroom situation a teacher should proceed with the demonstration slowly so that all the pupils may easily grasp the details, and whenever possible, involve pupils in the demonstration.

Discussion method

Apart from lecture method, another type of method of teaching is known as discussion method. This is the type of method of teaching where a teacher gives the all class or different groups within the class. The teacher can just give a topic to the class or a group to discuss.

Advantages

The following are the advantages of discussion methods.

- It helps to clarify the difficulties as rising from the lesson.
- It helps to develop students with various skills and abilities. E.g. skills and abilities such as critical and logical thinking.
- It helps those who are shy to overcome shyness.
- It encourages pupils to research more about the given topic.
- A lot of work can be covered by a group if topics are different.

Disadvantages and these include;

- Sometimes learners may not understand the topic fully.
- If the discussion methods are used constantly, the teacher became lazy such that he/she cannot prepare anything to teach the pupils.
- Slow learners do not discussion in that, they may not participate much.
- It promotes nose through loud discussion and hence disturbs other classes.
- Discussion method is applicable in the following subjects

For discussion method to be improved, the teacher should be able to control the learners, this is because if the groups are not controlled, it can result in the nosily discussion which can disturb others class. However, the teacher should make sure that he/she goes through the groups to guide the learners when help is needed. In addition to this, the teacher should make sure that in every group they are representatives who will be able to control the group.

PANEL METHOD.

This is when students are selected as panelists to discuss a given topic. Each panelist is free to air his/her views on the issue or certain aspects of the issue. There should be a moderator who gives turns to people who ask on what the panelist said. Address the moderator and in turn the moderator applies to the panelists to speak. Panelists must be given enough time to research on the topic before they come to discuss.

Advantages

The advantages of this teaching strategy are that:

- It encourages Students to research for information and develop skills for public address.
- Experts present different opinions.
- Can provoke better discussion than a one person discussion.
- Frequent change of speaker keeps attention from lagging.
- Personalities may overshadow content .

Disadvantages of this method are that:

- When there is no moderator who should give turns to people who ask on what the panelists said.
- Experts are often not effective speakers.
- Subject may not be in logical order.
- Not appropriate for elementary age students.
- Logistics can be troublesome.
- Teacher coordinates focus of panel, introduces and summarizes.
- Teacher briefs panel.

Synthetic Method

Synthetic method is another type of method which is used in teaching. This method proceeds from known to unknown. However, this is the type of method where by a teacher put things together which are apart. In short synthetic method is the type of method of putting together known bits of information to reach the point where unknown information becomes obvious and true.

Advantages

Synthetic method has the following advantages.

- It is a short and elegant method.
- It glorifies memory of the learners.
- It suits the teacher.
- It follows the same process as given in the text book.

Disadvantages

Disadvantages of synthetic methods are;

- It leaves much doubt in the mind of the learners.
- It offers no explanations for them.
- Learners become perplexed when new problem is put on them.
- It does not provide full understanding.
- There is no scope of discovery and thinking in this method.
- Home work and memory work are likely to become heavy for the learners.

For this method to be successful the teacher should show the learner on how to go with it and he must also motivate them. On the other hand, the teacher should show ways of answering the give work when the learners are at home.

Peer-Tutoring Method.

This type of method is where a teacher selects learners who perform well to tutor other who are having difficulties with the lesson. This method is more applicable in colleges, universities and other higher learning institutions.

Advantages

- Merits of peer-tutoring It develops a friendly relationship between the tutor and the tutee.
- It develops good communication skills between the tutor and the tutee.
- It makes students who tutor other usually learn to be responsible people.
- It helps both tutor and tutee to perform well in classroom work.
- The situation becomes impressive.
- The syllabus can be covered in a short period of time.

Demerits of peer- tutoring.

- It leaves some stone unturned for the learners
- At times they are no respect between the tutor and the tutee because they think that they are of the same age.
- Experimentation is totally neglected.
- They are no opportunity for other students to discover and find out facts for

For this method to be effective, a teacher must select tutor within the class. This we make the learners to feel comfortable with the tutor reason why, they in the same line.

Programmed Teaching Method

Programmed teaching method is a technique of teaching in a sequence of controlled steps, sometimes referred to as programmed learning; it is the product of a careful development process resulting in a reproducible sequence of instructional events, which has been demonstrated to produce measurable and consistent learning by students. It is mostly related with teaching using mechanical devices which are employed to present systematically a programmed sequence of instruction to a student. For instance tapes, modules and computers

Advantages

The **Advantages** of programmed learning as a teaching method are that:

- Most programs are self-paced.
- Students who can work rapidly are not held back, and those who need to work more slowly have a chance to master each stage of a program before moving on to the next stage.
- Individual progress can be continuous and the overall efficiency of the system becomes quite high.
- Programmed learning can dramatically increase a student's access to information.
- The program can adapt to the abilities and the preferences of the individual student and increase the amount of personalized instruction a student receives.
- Many students benefit from the immediate responsiveness of modules, tape and computer interactions and appreciate the self-paced and private learning environment.
- Moreover, if using computer learning experiences often engage the interest of students, motivating them to learn and increasing independence and personal responsibility for education.

Disadvantages

- It is difficult to assess the effectiveness of a student.
- Subjects that involve abstract reasoning and problem-solving processes cannot be very effective learned.
- On the other hand poorly designed programmed learning can dehumanize or regiment the educational experience and thereby diminish student interest and motivation.

- Other disadvantage of this method is the difficulty and expense of implementing and maintaining the necessary learning systems.

This method can be improved in many ways. The teacher must design the programmed before using it, this is because and when he is doing it in the classroom it may bring disturbances among the learners.

Project Method of Teaching

Project method of learning is more of a task or planned program of work that requires a large amount of time, effort, and planning to complete. it is a task given to a learner of group of learner to supplement and apply classroom strategies in working out the project given. Usually the project given is guided by the teacher, but the goals are designed by the learner based on his or her background of knowledge and experience. The role of the teacher under this method is simply to encourage the learner and guide them as they proceed.

Advantages

- Give learner experience in planning and organization
- Provides a natural approach of learning
- Creativity freedom of exposure co-operation and imitative

Disadvantage

- It is expensive and it takes a lot of time and effort in competition in comparison of what is learnt
- It is had to choose topics that are of interest to the learner
- It is difficult to maintain order and discipline when the projection is been done difficult to schedule the project

The Montessori Method of Teaching

The Montessori Method stresses the development of initiative and self-reliance by permitting children to do by them the things that interest them, within strictly disciplined limits Montessori educational method of teaching is based on giving children freedom in a specially prepared environment, under the guidance of a trained director Under this method it is stressed that leaders of the classroom be called directors rather than teachers because their main work is to direct the interests of children and advance their development. According to Montessori, when a child is ready to learn new and more difficult tasks, the director should guide the child from the outset so that the child does not lose interest.

Advantages

- It has immense value in bringing about peace in the learning environment
- this method stresses the importance of education as the 'armament of peace learners learn willingly without being forced the classroom leader the teach in this case has little or no problem in teaching as every one has interest in the content

Disadvantages

- it is difficult to teach basing on the interest of learner as they may have various interest other content may not be taught when learner has no interest in them
- its time consuming and needs lot of effort in preparing that which learner

Question And Answer Method

This method involves posing the question to the learners in order to promote thinking and understanding. It is informal assessment which is used with group of learners as a way of ascertaining the existing level of what learner have acquired from the previous material learnt or even in what there are yet to learn.

Advantages

- learners are motivated as they fell they are part and parcel of the learning
- misconceptions may be identified at the early stage and be rectified
- can help in building from simple to complex
- feedback of quality learning is determined by the response you get from the learners
- it stimulate the learners
- maintain concentration

Disadvantages

- A minority of learners may participate
- Careful planning may be required hence time consuming
- it demoralize the teacher after teaching you realize that nothing has been taught

Debate Method of Teaching

Debate is closely related to discussion method but it tends to have more rule regarding procedures. Debate method of teaching often has two arguments and both sides of argument would be helpful and learners may benefit from the exploration of fellow learners.

Advantages

- all learner are made to participate
- it motivate learner to study harder in quest of wanting to bit the opponent
- learner adopt the attitude of wanting to take a leading role
- good for continuous issues
- learners presentation skill are enhanced
- it creates a good class team work

Disadvantages

- A minority of learner may do most of the work
- It is time consuming as learner would need enough time for preparation and practice.
- It is learner centered hence it is reliable to have more of less baked information which would not be good for fellow learner.

Story Telling Method of Teaching

Story Telling Method of Teaching is another way in which learners can learn vast amounts of information by listening to others. Learning through the spoken word is similar to observational learning, because it allows people to learn not simply from their own experiences, but also from the experiences of others. For example, by listening to a teacher story about walking in busy streets alone, children can learn to avoid busy streets and to cross the street at crosswalks without first experiencing any positive or negative consequences.

Advantage

- It creates the ability in learners of Concept formation
- it enables learners to be sharp in thinking as they connect what is narrated to real life situation
- It saves both time and efforts
- learners learn a large portion of what they know through listening

Disadvantages

- Certain concept may be misapplied where they are not supposed to be applied.
- learners have little activities in story telling as they are there to listen only
- it may be boring hence learners fails to learn anything fro the story told

Deductive Method

It's a process of reasoning in which reasons are given in support of a claim. The reasons or justifications are called the premises of the claim and the claim they purport to justify is called the conclusion. In a correct or valid deduction the premises support the conclusion in such a way that it would be impossible for the premises to be true and for the conclusion to be false. In this deduction differs sharply from induction, because induction draws a conclusion in which the truth of the premises does not guarantee the truth of the conclusion. This method can be used in mathematic in proving the answer given at the end of computation.

Advantages

- It proves the fact basing on a clear elaborations
- it does not change
- it supports all true theory which can be proven.
- it enhances speed and efficiency in solving problems.
- it glorifies the memory as students have to memories a considerable number of formulae
- its drawbacks are. It is very difficult for a beginner to understand abstract formulae.
- It is not preceded by a number of concrete instances.
- it is not suitable for the development of thinking, reasoning and discovery.

Memory becomes more important than understanding and intelligence and that is educationally unsound.

Inductive Teaching Method

According to Hume (1748), this is a process of drawing a conclusion about an object or event that has yet to be observed or occur, on the basis of previous observations of similar objects or events. For example, after observing year after year that a certain kind of weed invades our yard every December, we may conclude that next December our yard will again be invaded by the weed; or having tested a substantially large sample of coffee makers, only to find that each one of them has a faulty fuse, we conclude that all the coffee makers in the batch are defective. In these cases we infer or reach a conclusion based on observations. The observations or assumptions on which we base the inference— the annual appearance of the weed, or the sample of coffee makers with faulty fuses—constitute the premises or assumptions

Advantages

- The laws of nature governing causes and effects are uniform followed up
- We can presume that a sufficiently large number of observed objects give us grounds to attribute
- Something to another object we have not yet observed.
- Induction raises important questions for teachers whose concern is to provide a basis of assessment it proves science conclusions be correct

Disadvantages

- they is struggled with the question of what justification
- it takes for granted induction's common assumptions that the future will follow the same patterns as the past
- The whole population behaves roughly basing on randomly chosen sample which may not represent others
- Nothing guarantees that simply because induction has worked in the past it will continue to work in the future.

- Justification are all assumptions, therefore it may raises the problem when the same fails in the other similar experiment it is tempting to try to justify induction by pointing out that inductive reasoning is commonly used in both everyday life.

Case-Based Teaching Method

In case-based teaching, students analyze case studies of historical or hypothetical situations that Involve solving problems and/or making decisions. Kardos& Smith (1997: 88) defined a case in the context of education as —an account of an education activity, event or problem containing some of the background and complexities actually encountered by an educationist. A case is a complete narrative of a problematic situation, how people dealt with it, and what the outcomes were. Students may be called on to study the case ahead of time and be prepared to discuss it in class, but the same may be said of any traditional lecture-based approach that incorporates questioning and answer.

Advantages

- Research cases can be useful for illustrating appropriate, typical, or exemplary decision making Lundeberg et al. [89] reported that, the use of case studies enhanced students' ability to recognize multiple perspectives
- The use of cases develops students' ability to identify relevant issues
- Cases improves students' reasoning and problem-solving skills
- Cases tend to be relatively well structured, rich contextual details are provided, and students are called on to apply material that is already somewhat familiar.

Disadvantages

- It's not good for teaching critical thinking and decision-making skills, since in those cases the thinking has already been done, the decisions made, and the outcomes determined and given to the students.
- Instruction based on the use of such cases cannot be considered inductive student are reluctant as they just listen and make mere decision basing on the story
- How It Can Be Improved To improve the use of case study teaching method a teacher must follow the following steps Review of the case content, statement of the problem, collection of relevant information, development of alternatives, evaluation of alternatives, selection of a course of action, and evaluation of solutions, and possibly review of actual case outcomes.

Project-Based Method of Teaching

Project-based teaching begins with an assignment to carry out one or more tasks that lead to the Production of a final report. The culmination of the project is normally a written and oral report summarizing the procedure used to produce the product and presenting the outcome.

Advantages

- Teachers fairly choose projects which helps maintain a focus on course and curriculum objectives.
- The students have nearly complete autonomy to choose their project and their approach to it.
- Students have the autonomy to choose their own project, formulations and strategies, which increases their motivation.
- Project-based learning may effectively reach students whose learning styles are poorly suited to a traditional lecture-based classroom environment learning is central to the course, it focuses on central concepts and principles of the discipline
- A project typically has a broader scope and may encompass several problems

Disadvantages

- Students have a less complete mastery of discipline fundamentals
- Some of students may be unhappy over the time and effort required by projects
- Students may experience interpersonal conflicts particularly with teammates who fail to pull their weight If the project work is done entirely in groups, some students may be less well equipped to work independently
- There are difficulties to accentuate the differences between strong and weak students requires acquisition of some new knowledge rather than being straightforward applications of existing knowledge How it can be improved Teachers should guide students to see connections between their current project and what they have learned previously.
- They should also prepare students to fill in gaps in content knowledge when a need arises, taking into account the fact that such gaps may be more likely to arise in project-based learning than in conventional lecture-based instruction.

Problem-Based Teaching Method

Problem-based teaching technique is when students are confronted with an open-ended, ill structured, authentic problem to be solved in teams or to identify learning needs and develop a viable solution, with instructors acting as facilitators rather than primary sources of information

Advantages

- Class time may be devoted to Groups reporting out their progress on previous learning issues and listing their current learning issues and plans of work
- Information on certain issues are dealt with by all groups, clarifying common Difficulties, and suggesting additional learning issues
- A well-designed problem guides students to use course content and methods, illustrates fundamental principles, concepts, and procedures
- It induces the students to infer those things for themselves instead of getting them directly from the instructor
- Engages the students in the types of reflection and activities that lead to higher-order learning Problems may Students may acquire more knowledge in the short term when instruction is conventional
- Students taught with PBL retain the knowledge they acquire for a longer period of time. it enhances students' retention and ability to apply material

Disadvantages

- There is very little formal class time if any, because students work on problems in groups during class.
- Time consuming, as the instructor moves from group to group during class, asking questions and probing for understanding.
- Different levels of external guidance may be required by a faculty member or a designated tutor, or responsibility for the work may be taken by the groups themselves in self-directed, interdependent, small group problem-based learning.

Team Teaching Method

Team teaching involves a group of instructors working purposefully, regularly, and cooperatively to help a group of students of any age learn. Teachers together set goals for a course, design a syllabus, prepare individual lesson plans, teach students, and evaluate the results. They share insights, argue with one another, and perhaps even challenge students to decide which approach is better.

Advantages

- Teamwork improves the quality of teaching as various experts approach the same topic from different angles
- Teacher strengths are combined and weaknesses are remedied

- Working in teams spreads responsibility, encourages creativity, deepens friendships, and builds community among teachers
- Poor teachers can be observed, critiqued, and improved by the other team members in a nonthreatening, supportive context.
- The evaluation done by a team of teachers will be more insightful and balanced than the introspection and self-evaluation of an individual teacher.
- Teachers complement one another.
- They share insights, propose new approaches, and challenge assumptions.
- They learn new perspectives and insights, techniques and values from watching one another.

Disadvantages

- It requires more time in planning and more efforts of skilled management
- it demands willingness to risk change and even failure, humility, open-mindedness, imagination, and creativity
- Some teachers do not want to risk humiliation and discouragement at possible failures.
- Some fear they will be expected to do more work for the same salary
- Team teaching is not always successful.
- Some teachers may have a rigid personality types or may be wedded to a single method.
- Others are unwilling to share the spotlight or their pet ideas or to lose total control.
- Team teaching makes more demands on time and energy
- Rethinking the courses to accommodate the team-teaching method is often inconvenient.

Direct Teaching Method

Through direct teaching methods, informal education, parents and elders can teach children the skills and roles they would need to know. These lessons eventually form the moral codes that governess behavior.

Advantages

- Very specific learning targets
- Students are told reasons why content is important - helps to clarify lesson objective
- Relatively easy to measure student gains
- Is a widely accepted instructional method
- Good for teaching specific facts and basic skills

Disadvantages

- Can stifle teacher creativity
- Requires well-organized content preparation and good oral communication skills
- Steps must be followed in prescribed order
- May not be effective for higher-order thinking skills, depending on the knowledge base and skill of the teacher How it can be improved
- Content must be organized in advance and Teachers should have information about student prerequisites.

Concetric Method.

This method implies widening of knowledge just as concentric circles go on extending and widenin. For example, an elementary knowledge is given in the introductory year, something more is taught in the next year, something more is still added in the subsequent year and so on. However this method is applicable in the universities, colleges and other higher of learning institutions.

Advantages

- It is a suitable system of arrangements because its opposite is highly unpsychological.
- It enables the teacher to do a portion of a topic according to the receptivity of learners.
- It does not allow the teaching to become dull.
- The learners get as much as they can grasp.
- And its drawbacks are follows. If the portion is too long, the interest is likely to flag.
- If the portion is too short, it is likely to make any lasting or permanent impression on the learner's mind.
- It may prove harmful.

Role Playing Teaching Method

Role-playing is trying to act the way one would act when given a certain position. Student acts or plays a certain role in a group; this method of learning can be employed at all levels of education. In role-playing student make mistakes without feeling threatened by the situation. Those who participate in role-playing maintain relationship and the teacher clearly define the problem which the group is to role-play. The relevant problem may be solved; this method can be applicable when teaching art and music in schools.

Advantages

- Introduces problem situation dramatically
- provides opportunity for students to assume roles of others and thus appreciate another point of view Allows for exploration of solutions
- Provides opportunity to practice skills

Disadvantages

- Some students may be too self-conscious
- Not appropriate for large groups
- Can be time consuming to set up and execute
- How it can be improved Teacher has to define problem situation and roles clearly; they must give very clear instructions and must have back up activities in case of problems.

Text Book Teaching Method

Parker, (1990: 190) defines a text book as: "A collection of knowledge, concepts, and principles of a selected topic or course, it's usually written by one or more teachers, college professors, or education experts who are authorities in a specific field" Textbook is likens to any tool, it can only be consider goods basing on the person using it.—Just like a hammer in the hands of a competent carpenter can be used to create a great cathedral or an exquisite piece of furniture, in the hands of someone else, the result may be a rundown shack or a rickety bench.Thus we must remember, no textbook is perfect, no textbook is complete. It is but one resource at our disposal to be used as a blueprint, a guidebook, or an outline. Mckeachi, (1994: 405) asserted that, —It's important to remember that a textbook is just one tool, perhaps a very important tool, in your teaching arsenal. Sometimes, teachers over-rely on textbooks and don't consider other aids or other materials for the classroom. Some teachers reject a textbook approach to learning because the textbook is outdated or insufficiently covers a topic or subject area". As teachers, we all need to make many decisions, and one of those is how you want to use the textbook, as good as they may appear on the surface.

Advantages

- Textbooks are especially helpful for begging teachers, the material to be covered and the design of each lesson are carefully spelled out in detail.
- Textbooks provide organized units of work.
- A textbook gives you all the plans and lessons you need to cover a topic in some detail.

- A textbook series provides you with a balanced, chronological presentation of information.
- Textbooks are a detailed sequence of teaching procedure that tells you what to do and when to do it.
- There are no surprises—everything is carefully spelled out.
- Textbooks provide administrators and teachers with a complete program.
- The series is typically based on the latest research and teaching strategies.
- Good textbooks are excellent teaching aids. They're a resource for both teachers and students.

Disadvantages

- Students only see one perspective on a concept or issue
- Textbook may be old or outdated; hence Information shared with students may not be current or relevant.
- Textbook questions tend to be low level or fact-based
- Textbook questions tend to be low level or fact-based, leading to students assume that learning is simply a collection of facts and figures.
- Textbook doesn't take students' background knowledge into account
- Teacher does not tailor lessons to the specific attributes and interests of students
- Reading level of the textbook is too difficult
- The textbook has all the answer to all the questions hence students tend to see learning as an accumulation of correct answers
- Students cannot read or understand important concepts

How it can be improved

A teacher must involve problem-solving activities, higher-level thinking questions, and extending activities, Ask higher-level questions and provide creative thinking and problem-solving activities. Provide students with lots of information sources such as trade books, CD-ROMS, Websites, and Encyclopedias'

Symposium Teaching Method

The plural form of this word is the symposia; symposium teaching method is similar or is closely related to discussion teaching method. The major distinction is that in a symposium each presenter is given a different work to present on. In a symposium when the question is posed it is specifically addressed to the presenter of the topic and not to the house at large.

Advantages

- It usually keeps individual attention
- it provide opportunities for independent student investigation in a wide range of a topic
- Provides opportunity to practice personal skills
- When used in direct relationship to a lesson objective, can provide a stimulating experience for all individual Students participate in the symposium students share experiences
- it helps student to relate their learning to real experiences and current problems
- It helps individual students to reflect on what has been given to present.

Disadvantages

- Some students may be too self-conscious, thus difficulties in coming out
- Not appropriate for large groups
- Can be time consuming to set up and execute
- Distractions happen all too easily
- Students working independently can easily lose focus of lesson topic
- Audience is often passive Learning is difficult to determine as the presenter progresses Communication

How It Be Improved

A Teacher must selects issue which are of the learners level of understanding and he must be ready to intervene when the process is hopelessly bogged down.

Dramatization Teaching Method

This is when teachers prepare a script for students in advance and students are given enough time opportunity to rehearse. This method helps students to experience and practice what they are learning. A good amount of caution is needed when organizing a drama

Advantages

- It Give an overview to explain the certain concept easily
- It develops in student the ability to Set up the scenario rules, roles, procedures, and types of decisions, goals and scoring
- Students give feedback and it is easy to evaluate the performance and decision-making
- You can easily Clarify misconceptions
- Enable students to take on and maintain their role as they interact with others in the drama
- It helps students to explore relationships between fictional and real worlds.

Disadvantages

- Difficulties in analyzing and evaluating the learning
- Difficulties in identifying students perceptions, difficulties and insights
- Student may find problem in relating some action with 'real' world Challenge in observing students during the drama play

How it can be improved

To improve this method further the teacher must let student to describe what they have experienced, identify reason and think through major concepts, issues and/or themes that emerged from the experience, analyze what this means for themselves and their roles. Encourage students to explore relationships between fictional and real worlds. Encourage students to reflect on how the drama relates to the world outside. Invite students to share reactions and observations in and out of role.

Collaboration Teaching Method

Collaboration allows students to actively participate in the learning process by talking with each other and listening to other points of view. Collaboration establishes a personal connection between students and the topic of study and it helps students think in a less personally biased way. Group projects and discussions are part of this teaching method.

Advantages

- Useful in assessing student's abilities to work as a team, leadership skills, or presentation abilities
- In collaboration pupils react to a specific problem within a structured environment
- It is useful for promoting expression of attitudes, opinions and values
- Fostering participation and developing empathy
- Can be excellent to help a group of learners think creatively of new ideas to solve difficult problems.

Disadvantages

- It might also be time-consuming as it requires a considerable amount of preparation
- It would demand Teacher to talk with the learners on a one to one basis whom he has identified with weakness hence more effort is needed it does not really reinforces learning in realistic and meaning full way it present a

threatening learning environment to students who are not bold.

How It Can Be Improved

To improve Collaborative method we need to take a variety of forms, such as fishbowl discussions. After some preparation and with clearly defined roles, a discussion may constitute most of a lesson, with the teacher only giving short feedback at the end of the lesson.

Testing Teaching Method

Often times testing is used as teaching technique. Tests provide student opportunity to learn. After students have written a test the teacher should mark and discuss parts of the test were much of student had not fared well then re-teach those parts. Sometimes a teacher can set take home test where students are given an opportunity to read, probe and find answers to questions. by so doing it help them find same thing to read at home.

Advantages

- Students learn a lot from take home tests
- Take home tests help to cover any content which was left hanging due to time constrain
- It gives learners experience in planning and organization of answers
- Provides a natural approach of learning

Disadvantages

- It needs a lot of time and effort in compiling the questions from different past papers or class notes
- It is hard to choose questions that are of learners level
- Sometimes during the tests it is difficult to evaluate who have understood as others may be coping
- Difficulty also to schedule the test.

How it can be improved

Teacher must set test rules to guard student against copping, he must have also Computing skills required for preparations of tests. Most effective teachers prepares test for themselves and do all the typing to avoid leaking.

Dictation Teaching Method

In this context dictation method can be define as, type of teaching where a teacher or facilitator read out to the pupils and the pupils writes down the notes. This method is mostly used in lower basic classes; it plays an important role as in the middle basic

Advantages

- Enables learners to spell properly
- Improves the mental capability of the learners
- Enables them to be good writers and remember every facet of the word
- Reduces boredom within the learners
- It enables learners to socialize with the facilitator(s)
- It arouses the interest of the learners to be psychologically ready for a lesson

Disadvantages

- Difficulty for the learners to express themselves in terms of the spellings
- Some find it too difficult to be psychologically ready for a lesson
- Some learner fails to be free and feels neglected.
- Difficulty for them to understand certain words
- Time consuming for a tutee as he would be required to repeat some words.

Telling Method

Telling method according to Marthur (1962:110), is the pedagogical method whereby the teacher makes a brief oral presentation of some fact of concept of educational significances, it is a method often resorted to by teachers for supplying the students with information above events, incidents and simple facts.

Advantages

- Telling is particularly useful as a teaching method when:
- Introducing new topics
- Summarizing work
- Reviewing work
- Supplementing information furnished by students and text books.
- Developing the work of the class
- Giving illustrative talks
- Giving inspiration talks.
- Introducing important incidental information.

Disadvantages

- It is not possible to elicit the information for the students or make them active participants in the learning process.
- The presentation may not be logical if the teachers (presenters) have got inadequate imagination, accurate and wide knowledge.
- The presentation may be boring if the presenters have not collected adequate information and facts on the topic at hand.

Nevertheless this method is almost applicable in all subjects. To enhance it, every teacher should know that telling is an art. As alluded to, a teacher should have variety of facts of the story to tell the class.

Analytic Method

According to Montessori (1917:211) defined analysis as, —the breaking up of the problem in hand so that it ultimately gets connected with something.I In other words, it is the process of unfolding of the problems or conducting its operation to know its hidden aspects. For example, this method requires us to start with, what we have to find out. Then we think of further steps and possibilities which may connect the unknown with known and lead us to find out the desired result. Thorndike says that, —all the highest performance of the mind is analysis. Analytical method can be used in the teaching and learning of mathematics and other related objects therefore can be improved by encouraging students to do some research in their learning subjects.

Advantages

- Analytic method is logical, leaves no doubts and convinces the learner.
- It is suitable method for understanding and discovering.
- The steps, in its procedure, are developed in a general manner. Each step has its reason and justification.
- The student is throughout faced with questions and this increases his power at every step.

Disadvantages

- It is a lengthy method.
- It is difficult to acquire efficiency and speed with this method. It may not be applicable to all the topics.

Memorization Method

This is a method of teaching which involves an act of using repetition to memorize facts. It is probably used in science or in mathematics in which questions, formulae even answers at time are printed on the flash cards to help learners remember information easily. Therefore, it provides to learners the ability to recall information randomly. However, to enhance this act, the teacher should be resourceful in one 17 sense that he must ensure that any topic taught should have flash cards containing main points of the overall topic.

Advantages

- It helps learners build language skills.
- It develops the learners learning skills.
- It improves learners understanding of literature.
- It improves learner's memory.
- Learners can have a firm basis for progressing to more complicated problem-solving skills.

Disadvantages

- Very little information can be memorized at a time.
- It creates and promotes laziness among pupils.
- Memorizing is disappointing in that it can only last for a short period of time.
- It limits learners from exploring or doing research.

Interview Method

This is type of teaching and learning method whereby learners are taught and imparted with techniques of collecting information by asking a number of questions. It is usually applied in research project especially in agricultural projects. One way to improve this method is when 18 Interviewing, the interviewee should be interrogated with both open and closed questions. Other than this one, learners should be acquainted with interview skills.

Advantages

- It encourages interactions between and among people especially an interviewer and an interviewee.
- It improves creativity as the learners will make a report out of the interview.
- It gives adequate time to prepare questions to ask.
- It provides a logic way of doing work.

Disadvantages

- It is time consuming.
- A learner may get the wrong information.
- Some people would not be willing to talk to them.
- Some learners cannot open up, hence the teacher or an interviewer will not get what he/she required.

Play Way Method

Yoakam et al (1957:59), define play-way method as, —a teaching method that introduces elements of happiness and satisfaction in form of games and prepares the minds of the learners to express fully to him or herself. Play-way method can be utilized in the teaching of various subjects of the school curriculum to make them lively and interesting. In the teaching of languages play way can include dramatization of interesting anecdotes and plays, debate, discussion, speeches, spelling games and story games. As for teaching social studies, a number of play way devices can be used for instance, dramatics, pageants and tableau, charts, models, pictures and so forth. Basically, the success and improvement of play- way depends upon the hard labour put in by the teacher. The use of play- way can, in no way, be taken as the line of least resistance to which a teacher can succumb, but it is a whole- hearted application to an arduous task of facilitating the learning process in a natural and interesting manner.

Advantages

- The application of play principle is a great force in education in that play is a wonderful motivator, because it is interesting.
- Work wedded to joy is work at its best.
- Play provides training in self-discipline and self-advancement through self-education.
- The harmony of work and play keeps the child fully absorbed in work. 20
- Play- way is the best way of learning.

Disadvantages

- Teacher may fail to achieve some objective because some pupils may be shy.
- It is time consuming.
- It requires a proper and formal guidance by the teacher.
- If the class is big, it can bring commotions.

Home work method

Assignment of homework is one of the forms of adult-centred or teacher-centerd methodology. This method of teaching has great educational benefits. It is argued, if learning is worthwhile, it should not be confined merely to the hours students spend in the classroom. This method is applied in subjects like science, English, geography, History and many others. Moreover, the syllabus for different classes in different subjects is so heavy that, it will be impossible to cover it so to improve this method a teacher should always at least give an aid of homework to learners on each topic covered in a day.

Advantages

- It gives opportunity to pupils to plan and perform, then work independent with the guidance and help from the teacher.
- It is a valuable means of study without the restrictions of class work and supplements the teaching work done in the class.
- Pupils' ability in the letter use of books and resources outside school, improves.
- It involves much repetition that is essential for fixing the lesson taught in the class.
- It develops the moral and intellectual qualities of self-reliance, self-direction and initiative in grappling unaided with the problem arising from the work.
- It stimulates in the pupils voluntary effort to follow up the study of subjects that appear to his interests and accustoms him to revise and consolidate the work done in the school.
- It establishes a habit of reading regularly- a habit which goes a long way in the pursuits of knowledge.

Disadvantages

- There is the risk of homework becoming oppressive and inflicting incalculable moral, intellectual and physical injury on the pupils and thus self defeating.
- It gets students to have outside of class experiments that will support class learning and still not arouse their rebellion or 27 stifle any interest they have in learning.
- Many teachers use homework as a means of punishing the pupils.
- Conflicts between pupils and teachers may arise.

Simulation Method

Simulation method can best be defined as role-playing method of teaching in which the process of teaching is displayed artificially an effort is made to practice some important skills of communication through this technique. The pupil-teacher and the students stimulate the particular role of a person or actual life-situation. The whole programme, thus, becomes training in role perception and roleplaying. It can be useful in civic education and other related subjects. Simulation method work in a group to improve this method a teacher should ensure to come up with groups each comprising of about three to five individual. One trainee for instance; in English Literature acts as an actor and the other provides the spontaneous setting for practicing specific patterns of behavior. The smaller the stimulated social skill training group, the more practice per person when assignments are related.

Advantages

- Stimulation establishes a setting where theory and practice can be combines.
- Stimulation required the teacher to be active participants in the process.
- There is no risk involved. The decision are made and carried out without physical or physiological harm to pupils.

Disadvantages

- Need for many simulators
- If classroom teaching is to be carried on with this method, a lot of time is required.
- There is also a minimum of feedback sequence to choose from.
- Analysis approach to problem – solving using this method becomes distinct.

Seminar Method

This is a teaching method which is mostly imperative to pupils. It encourages learners to do a research on a particular topic and afterwards, present their findings to the rest of the learners in the classroom. This method can be used in subjects such as geography, commerce and history. It can be improved by ensuring that learners take the serious active part in doing a research and a teacher should provide formal guidance in which they shall go about.

Advantages

- Learners are given chances to interrogate their peers on their findings.
- Learners are involved in participations in the study.
- Learners know what to study, since they are given an opportunity to choose topics to study of the own interest.
- It gives presentation responsibility to the learners.

Disadvantages

- It demands for a clear summary of the issues presented at the end of it.
- Assessment of learners becomes difficult.
- Some learners may not be ready or willing to participate due to fear, shy and other factors.

Field Trip

This is one of the teaching methods in which a number of learners taught on a particular topic are taken out of their normal learning situations to a real-life situation where realism is essential to reinforce learning. It is mostly used in history and Geography subjects. One way to improve it is by planning and coordinating all real resources before time so that destructions are minimized.

Advantages

- Learners are able to witness the real objects.

- It aids memory.
- It is a realistic and live method.
- It provides a powerful link between theory and practice.
- It motivates learners to learning.

Disadvantages

- It is difficult to monitor students during visits.
- It is costly. iii. It consumes time.

Discovery Teaching Method

Discovery learning is an inquiry-based approach in which students are given a question to answer, a problem to solve, or a set of observations to explain, and then work in a largely self directed manner to complete their assigned tasks and draw appropriate inferences from the outcomes, —discovering‖ the desired factual and conceptual knowledge in the process. In the purest form of this method, teachers set the problems and provide feedback on the students' efforts but do not direct or guide those efforts.

Merits of Discovery Teaching Method

- Discovery learning can enhance students' retention of material
- Retention is improved more when the learning task is based on previously understood principles
- Teachers cover a small fraction of their prescribed content if students are required to discover everything for themselves
- Guided inquiry and discovery learning on the acquisition, transfer and retention of motor skills
- Discovery learning produces improved learning outcomes without requiring a major sacrifice of content.

Demerits of Discovery Teaching Method

- It's found not statistically significant because of differences in student scores on tests and lab reports
- Discovery learning does not enhance students' retention of material
- Retention is improved only when the learning task is based on previously understood principles

How it can be improved

What teachers should do to improve the use of discovery teaching method is apply a variant of discovery learning which is sometimes called —guided discovery‖ that involves the instructor providing some guidance throughout the learning process. Once this is done, the distinctions between discovery and guided inquiry or problem-based learning tend to disappear. Subjects applicable Mathematics, geography, history, and religious education

Modeling

Modeling is a type of visual aid for teaching as well as learning. It is a known fact that human brain absorbs more and understands better when visual aid facilitates explanation. This method works on three criteria - observing, retaining and replicating. The students learn more by observing the things and acquire it by imitating it time and again.

Drill Method

As its name, this method which is employed when it's necessary to repeat some information into the minds of the learners. This method can be employed to complement other methods.

Advantages

- It provides a learner with a focus on accuracy
- It provides a learner with intensive practical hearing and saying particular words or phrases.

- it provides a safe environment for learners to experiment with producing the language
- It helps the learners notice the correct form of pronunciation of a word or phrase

Disadvantages

- It is hard for learners to focus when done of too often
- learners who learn only by drill may get distracted and bored with practice drills, especially if they have already mastered the skills learners may not be truly learning

How To Improve The Method
This method can be made effective if the teacher he, himself is active in the way he does things and also by guiding the learners in order for them to understand fully.

Dogmatic Method
In this method of teaching of mathematics region is extremely emphasized. the rules and formulae are given to the class to cram the teacher tells the pupils what to do, what to observe, how to attempt and how to conlude.

Advantages

- The method saves time, energy and a good deal of loose or useless thinking
- it can be adopted with advantages at a stage when pupils are adequately advanced in material development
- it glorifies memory
- it promotes skill, efficiency, and speed in the solution of problems

Disadvantages

- The subject becomes dull and un interesting for the learners as mechanical method cannot promote interest most of the mechanically memorized information is likely to be forgotten soon the learners repeats and adopt other`s ideas and becomes a slave of the ideas of others

How To Improve It
The pattern as presented by the teacher should be strictly adopted and imitated by the learners

Creative Writing
Here students can learn through creative writing of which the teacher helps the learners to identify the problem or the issue involved through this method the learners may be able to solve problem or what they need to solve

ADVANTAGES

- It helps learners to develop fast thinking capabilities
- it accelerates and strengthen the learners natural creative problem solving ability and to stimulate a large number of good diverse ideas

DISADVANTAGES

- There is need for close supervision by the teacher especially on the topic to write
- it is time consuming for it requires the learner to research more on how to make his writing interesting

How To Improve It
In order to make this method effective the teacher should always be there to guide the learners on how to go about the writing and to come up with good results and develop a good writing skill

Historical/ Source Method

This is another activity method teaching history. According to this method, the pupils are expected to build up history with help of available source material. one of the most important skill the student learn through this method is the skill to use sources.

Advantages

- It develop a sense vividness and reality
- it can satisfy the curiosity of children on the question
- helps teacher to illustrate more important points in support of an oral lesson

Disadvantages

- It is not always for the teacher to have access to the sources
- utilization of the sources is not easy for the teacher
- the method is too complex and technical

How To Improve It

The teacher should give the learners a training in the alimentary knowledge of in stenography by teaching learners what is effected in a particular source for example a text book.

Socialised And Recitation Method

a basic structure of this approach, there must be an outline material to be covered, either in a text book or presented in other fashion. This method is therefore that learners presented with question designed to stimulate the mental activity of the class and to produce some kind of answer.

Advantages

- It trains the pupils for participation in social environment.
- Qualities of leaders are developed
- it promotes democracy in class
- it insures increased learning

Disadvantages

- It is time consuming
- produces monetary
- it permits a few pupils to dominate the discussion
- it is difficult to organize and manage the learners

How To Improve It

The teacher should ensure that socialization and recitation centers and a topic which is important from the point of view of the pupils.

Buzz Method

This method is very flexible such that it can not be narrowly defined. Therefore it is certainly applied whenever large assembly of people are divided into smaller groups of usually not less than three and not more than eight

Advantages

- The class confronts the subject matter first hand rather than passively received what a teacher
- shall say helps learner to quickly adapt the learning environment

Co-Operative Learning

This method involves small haterogenious student group working together to solve problems or complete a task to minimize their own and each other learning

Advantages

- Help improve higher self esteem
- helps improve social skills
- it also imparts a student`s ability to work co-operatively

Disadvantages

- It is time consuming
- some learners may not participate

How To Improve It

The method can be improved in a way that the teacher should plan adequately in order to meet the learner`s expectations.

Biographical Method

According to this method subjects are taught through biographies presented on a chronological order. The ideology behind this method is that great men represent their times. They influence historical movements and thus represents in their individual personality.

Advantages

- they solve the problem of motivation as the lesson becomes interesting
- acquaintance with the great and characters of the past creates a desire to be like them enabling

Disadvantages

- The theory great men represents b their times cannot be acceptedØ the method promotes hero worship

How It Can Be Improved

The teacher should select outstanding events or movements and individuals grouped around them. And also the teacher should be able to guide and translates the subject matter.

Topical Method Of Teaching

This amethod that keeps the topic intact, it is taken as a unified whole. mainly the method is based on the principles that any topic when begun should not left half done.

Advantages

- It offers the learners with full and whole hearted concentration on the topic at hand
- there is a coherence in the preparation of lessons in a classroom
- learners are actively involved by participation

Disadvantages

- Learners might lose interest in the topic if too ,long
- it does not provide any opportunity for revision

How It Can Be Improved

It can be improved by combining it with other teaching methods like concentric and questioning

Research Method

According to Allan (2003), defines research method as a kind of learning where learners use various methods and instruments of finding relevant information

Advantages of Research Method

- It enables the teacher to pass on their experiences of the application of research
- methodologies
- it equips learners with self discoveries

Disadvantages

- It is time consuming it is expensive for it requires enough sources
- A large group can be difficult to handle by one teacher

How To Improve

It can be an effective one if the teacher prepares adequately in order to show the learners what to observe and do.

Pneumonics Method

This is a teaching method that can be used to reach fact, labels, rules, and procedure. it can be done in form of music, rhythm when introducing the new topic

Advantages

- It improves learner`s ability to memorize content
- learners develop a zeal of singing and following the song
- pneumonic devices can be constructed without much hassle

Disadvantages

- It is time consuming
- some learners will just be singing for pleasure and not following the song`s meaning.

How It Can Be Improved

The teacher should ensure that he is equipped with the meaning of the songs so that learner can understand and make sense out of it. learners should be encouraged to sing the songs in order not to forget easily

Propaganda Teaching

Method Propaganda Teaching Method involves dissemination of ideas and information for the purpose of inducing or intensifying specific attitudes and actions. It is frequently accompanied by distortions of fact and by appeals to passion and prejudice and it is often thought to be invariably false or misleading. This view is relative, however. Although some propagandists may intentionally distort fact, others may present it as faithfully as objective observers. In Education, whatever is objective is a form of propaganda. The essential distinction lies in the intentions of the propagandist to persuade an audience to adopt the attitude or action he or she espouses

Advantages

- It clear all miscomputation
- It intensify specific attitudes and actions
- It persuades learners to adopt the attitude or action the teacher wants in them

Disadvantages

- It may sometimes distort fact by appeals of passion and prejudice thought invariably false or misleading teaching many learner are compelled to believe even that which is not true
- Teachers are made to teach centrally to what they believe without revealing the truth they know.

Assignment Teaching Method.

This is a teaching technique where a teacher gives work to the student to go and find solutions to the problems given.

Advantages

- It enables' a teacher to cover the work in a stipulated time with a given syllabus
- It enriches the student mind set
- It motivates the students when doing their work at personal level
- It brings about social relationships among the learners
- It enables the learners to meet up with new challenges when doing their assignments.
- It enables the learners to develop the culture or research-hence improving their memory

Disadvantages

- Its time consuming
- Expensive
- It brings boredoms to the learners who have a teachers learning syndrome

Methods of clinical teaching presentation

Introduction

Nursing education is a practice discipline. The students will learn the subject matter by doing the things and practicing the skills. Clinical teaching will provide the places where the actual clients are being cured for. Learning experiences require the presence of clinical instructor, guide, reinforce and correct the behavior of the learners

Definition

clinical teaching methods refer to the logical course of actions to accomplish particular educational goals in a specific environment in which students can get opportunities of learning outcomes.

Selection of methods

it should be based on expected outcomes, principles of teaching, learning and learners. Teaching strategies in clinical settings are unique.

Who can participate

various members of health team can take part in clinical teaching program such as doctors, head nurse, staff nurse and clinical instructor etc.

How to support these methods-

well planned ward teaching program provides a valuable contribution to the students. Educational objectives are clear to all members who are taking part in ward teaching. It should be4 an integral part of nursing curriculum.

Classification of the clinical teaching methods

There are various clinical teaching methods to make the learning more effective. Some of the most commonly used clinical teaching methods are as follows-

- Nursing care plan
- Nursing case study
- Bedside clinics
- Nursing rounds
- Nursing care conference

- Group conference
- Individual conference
- Demonstration and re-demonstration
- Process recording
- Clinical assignment

Nursing care plan

- The nursing care plan is used to provide a guide to patient care.
- Plan is made based on priority, as the nursing needs are vary from patient to patient and it should be based as per his need.
- Nursing care plan is a projected plan and is for immediate and future use.
- Nursing care plan helps students provide more competent and need based care.
- Students are required to write the care plan implement, evaluate and modify to meet the patients needs.
- Student can discuss the plan with the clinical instructor regarding intervention and rational for the care.

Role of teacher

- To guide the discussion.
- Correct any wrong concepts.
- Give additional information to meet the objectives.
- To evaluate the student's level of knowledge and skills and their actual applications in nursing.

Advantages

- Better nursing care d;ue to efforts of students.
- Student gain greater understanding of human psychology.
- It helps to understand the effects the disease on the patient and family.
- Student can learn problem solving approach.

Bedside clinic:

- It's a method of clinical teaching where patient's medical history and therapies are discussed in brief followed by identification of patient's problem.
- Bedside clinic is one of the most effective method of clinical teaching. New knowledge is acquired through observation and study of the actual patient.

Methods of bedside of clinics

- Clinic can be held at the bedside or can bring the patient to the classroom near the ward.
- Patient should have typical condition.
- Duration usually 30 minutes.
- Group of students should be small. (6-8).
- Make the patient comfortable.
- Prior permission should always be taken from patient.
- Patient may requested to talk about family, onset of disease and signs and symptoms.
- Patient not present for entire discussion.
- Nursing care, patient's problems and treatment therapies all to discussed before he is brought to ward classroom.

- Nothing should be done to hurt patient's feelings.
- Clinical instructor may lead the discussion.
- After this group interact with the patient and patient allowed to go to his bed.
- Topic summarized, important points emphasized and evaluation done by the clinical instructor.

Nursing rounds meaning

very important methods mainly used by ward sister, clinical instructor for clinical teaching. Large group of patients are discussed for their specific problems. Medical and nursing care given at bedside. This method helps us to know all the patients in ward. Their bed to bed discussion about patients problems and solutions.

Purposes

- To Encourage teaching among students about various cases in the ward.
- Enhances student knowledge about different patients.

Timings for nursing round

- should not interfere with the ward routine.
- It is not conducted during doctor's and time for patient's medical care.

How to conduct nursing rounds

- Usually conducted by ward sister, clinical instructor as they know each patient's problem more intimately.
- Students should be informed before hand.
- Bedside patient round should be stopped briefly for a short discussion about specific nursing problem.
- Instructor/ward sister may call upon any nurse to tell about the patient and nursing care given.
- Nursing round timings up to 40-50 minutes and attendance of all students are required.
- Whole ward/unit has to be covered in this brief weekly summary of nursing problem.

Values of nursing rounds

- Helps in arousing students interest to read the history of all patients, review disease conditions, medications, doses, actions and side effects etc.
- Encourage discussion among students about various cases in the ward.
- Head nurse/clinical instructor to test the student's knowledge of all the patients.
- No other type of round is substitute for nursing rounds.
-

Nursing care conference : how is it planned

- It is same as bedside clinic but patient usually not present.
- This method may be used when whole group well acquainted with the patient and the group have nothing to do for the patient.
- Group members must have opportunity to know patient, read patient history, progress notes, nurses notes and laboratory findings and the treatment of the diseases.

Group conference: definition

- It is a method of clinical teaching. Group of students and clinical instructor need for a discussion of patients problem. Group should not be more than 10-12 students. Each student can get a chance of participation.

Role of clinical instructor

- Clinical instructor act as a leader, she must be sensitive to the group for all things which show the attitude of the group members.
- She need to have patience and should not answer the questions too quickly, but wait for students answers.
- She should be able to guide the students.
- Correct wrong interpretations and should be given time to complete sentence.
- Subject/area should be closely related student's daily experience in the department.
- Students are guided in solving nursing problems.
- The success of this type of teaching depends upon the topic chosen for discussion.

Subject for group conference

- Orientation of a new students to the department.
- Nursing care needs of a particular patients or group of patients.
- Conference on nursing procedures, eg. Records, report writing, intake and output charting, preparing patient for surgery etc.
- Discussion on drugs, diets and treatments.
- Nursing projects and fields trips etc.
- Hospital house keeping, hospital routine etc.
- Proper handling of sophisticated equipments and instruments.

Values of group conference

- Most profitable methods of clinical teaching.
- It encourages active participation of each group members.
- Subject matter deal with proper guidance of clinical instructor.
- Group thinking and discussion awakens interest and appreciation.

Individual conference definition

- Individual conference is an interaction between teacher and a learner.
- It can be planned and unplanned.
- Such conferences are held in ward with the student and clinical instructor/ward sister.

Subject Matter

- Related to students nursing ability.
- Quality of work performance.
- Relating to students achievements.
- Test results written or practical.

Role of clinical instructor

- Listen to student's problems, difficulties regarding clinical experience.

- Give the chance to student to express her feelings.
- Effective and useful guidance to the student's based on her difficulties.
- Always respect the student as an individual.
- Discuss the student's problem and achievements.
- Try to alley he fear, anxiety and doubts.
- Be friendly informal and biased.
- For planned conference, student should be informed before hand.
- Place should free from interruptions, less noisy as privacy and allow the student to sit down so she feels more relaxed.

Values of individual conference

- It offers useful opportunities for teaching and learning.
- Student and instructor discuss particular problem.
- Student can know about her progress etc.
- Provides a sense of security.
- Excellent opportunity for an individual learning.

VII
Educational Media

Educational Media are the instructional techniques that facilitate learning. Media are the means of implementing those methods. Methods are the instructional techniques that facilitate learning. Media are the means of implementing those methods (as well as conveying the material to be learned). For example, methods include demonstrations, animations, examples, practice, and feedback.

Media include overhead slides, computers, video, workbooks, and instructors among others.

Methods

Methods refer to the way through which messages are conveyed to achieve a desired behavioral change in target audience.

Media

Media is the collective communication outlets or tools used to store and deliver information or data.

Classification of Methods and Media of Health Education

1. **Classification of Methods**

· **Individual Methods**

This method includes person – to – person or face – to – face communication which provides maximum opportunities for two – way flow of ideas, knowledge and information. There should be good interaction between the health educator and a client. **e.g. interview and counseling.**

· **Group Method**

This method involves a group of limited persons who need some kind of health education need about certain health problems. It is an effective way to give health education because it provides the audience the ample opportunities for question-answer and discussion. e. g. demonstration, group-discussion, role-playing, panel-discussion, study-trip, project assignment, symposium, case-study, mini-lecture, training and workshop etc.

· **Mass Method:**

This method usually includes a large number of heterogeneous people having various social strata i. e. from different location, culture and position. Because of its complexity, there is no opportunity for two-way communication. It is more beneficial when there is lack of resources and inadequate time. e. g. lecture or public speech, exhibition and campaign.

Typical methods of health EDUCATION

Lecture

This is the traditional classroom mode of instruction and usually refers to a formal presentation of information, concepts or principles by an individual. A lecture can be modified to include discussion, demonstration and application.

- **Guided Discussion**

This method is an instructor-controlled, interactive process of meeting performance objectives by sharing information and learner experiences in the classroom.

- **Demonstration**

The demonstration is the basic method for teaching psychomotor skills.

- **Case Study**

The case study method uses a detailed written description of a real or imaginary situation that can be analyzed and discussed by the learners.

- **Role-Playing**

In role-playing the learners act out a situation based on real life.

Selection of methods and media

In the selection of the instructional media, Romiszowski(1997) says that the main categories of factors that may influence the choice of media are:

1. **Task factors**– the type of objectives, and hence the type of learning activities which should be provided for the learner.

2. **Learner factors**– some learners may learn better from certain media than from others3. **Economics/availability factors**– this may limit the choice in practice

Importance of Health Education Methods

- Helps to disseminate health information and ideas to the audience.
- Motivate people to adopt healthy behaviors.
- They help to encourage for team approach in learning and solving health problems.
- Exhibition helps to develop creativity in learners.
- Methods like study trip enables students to relate what they have learnt in the classroom to reality of outside world.
- Some methods like group discussion , role play, workshop, symposium and brainstorming helps to interact with participants in the group

Effective ways of using methods:

(a) Plan well before the methods are used: What, why, when, where and how to use methods

(b) Plan of the physical facilities and audiences:

(c) Use methods according to the teaching learning situation and the target learners

(d) Follow the criteria of evaluation of the used methods

Educational aids /Media used in health education

The aids used for transmitting health education are the main constituent of the armamentarium of health education process

Auditory Aidss

Based on the principles of sound, electricity and magnetism

- Useful in reproducing any kind of words spoken and also helps in repeating the same
- examples;
- Megaphones
- Microphones
- Gramophone records and discs
- Tape records
- Phone
- Radios
- Sound amplifiers

Visual Aids

- Based on the principle of projection.
- Helps individuals to understand better.
- Examples are;
- Blackboards
- Slides
- Bulletin Boards
- Film Strip
- Flannel board
- Model
- Puppet
- Graphs and charts
- Flash Card
- overhead Projector
- Printed aids-textbook, newspaper and periodicals

Audio Visual aids

- Motion
- Picture
- Television

7 Rights of Audio Visual aids

- Right aid
- Right place
- Right way
- Right time
- Right people
- Right message
- Right extension worker

Functions of Audio Visual Aids
When properly used, audio visual aids contribute one or more of the following functions.

- Convey meaning clearly
- Capture attention, arouse and sustain interest
- Increase the correctness, clarity and effectiveness of the idea and skills being transferred
- Help in learning more, faster, and with thoroughness
- Help in remembering longer
- Reach more people, irrespective of their level of literacy, or language
- Save the instructor's time
- Reduce the possibility of misinterpreting concepts
- Clarify the relationship between material objects and concepts
- Supplement the spoken word – the combination of audio and visual stimuli is particularly effective since the two most important senses are involved
- Highlight the main points of the message clearly.

Limitations of Audio Visual Aids

- Learners may sometimes form distorted impressions, unless audio visual aids are supplemented with required explanations
- They may tempt the extension worker to narrow down his teaching to only a few big ideas, not giving the complete picture of a subject
- There is the possible risk of 'spectatorism' instead of the attitude of thoughtful enquiry. Some extension workers acquire the mistaken idea that they have little to do when audio visuals are used.

Audio aids are the instructional devices through which message can only be heard. It is said that we spend more than 50% of our time in hearing. This shows the importance of audio media in our life. Therefore, as an extension worker, it is necessary for you to understand important audio aids and their application in extension and development work.

Advantages

- Flexible, inexpensive, simple to use, and readily available.
- Recorded and used again and again - Editing and duplication is easy.
- Useful in individual, group, and mass teaching methods.
- Overcomes the illiteracy barrier.
- Audio messages are more dramatic than print messages.
- Portable and can be used in field situations.

Limitations

- The sequence of presentation is fixed.
- Comprehension of the presentation can be a constraint.
- The development of audio aids is time consuming.
- Storage and retrieval of audio tapes and records is tiresome. Important audio aids that are useful for extension work, along with their specific advantages and limitations, are discussed next for your understanding.

Tape Recorder

A tape recorder is suitable for extension work in meetings, training programmes, campaigns, recording radio programmes, etc.

Advantages

- Facilitates on-the-spot recording of sound.
- Helps in duplication and dissemination of sound.
- Recorded tape can be immediately played back without any processing.
- Helps in synchronization of sound with picture.
- Easy to operate and preserve.
- Low operational cost, as the same tape may be used again.

NON-PROJECTED VISUAL AIDS

Non projected visual aids are those aids which are used without projection.

Advantages

- Abundant and are easily obtainable.
- Requires no electricity and appropriate for low budget extension work.
- Not much artistic ability is required in the use of these visual aids.
- Useful in small group situations.
- Many of them can be converted into projected aids. For example, charts, flannel graphs, and flash cards can be photographed or scanned and converted into slides.
- Some of them can be projected through an opaque projector.

Chalkboard, or Blackboard

The chalkboard is probably the simplest, cheapest, most convenient, and widely used non projected visual aid in extension teaching. A black wooden board is mostly used, hence, it is also known as blackboard. However, ground glass, rollup materials, coloured in black, olive green, or blue may also be used. Roll-up materials are made of heavy cloth canvas coated with chalkboard paint. For extension teaching under field conditions, inward folding wooden boards or rollup materials are convenient. The chalkboard is suitable for use in lectures, training programmes, group meetings, etc. As one of the oldest aids to teaching known for the past four hundred years, the chalkboard is known for its ubiquitous presence in classrooms. It is a vehicle for a variety of visual materials.

Purpose Audio-Visual Aids

- To write important points to support oral presentation.
- To put illustrations for visualization of facts.
- Serve as base for recording learner's inputs and help them in practice.
- Serve as surface for displaying other non projected visuals such as photographs, charts, graphs, diagrams, etc.

Guidelines

- The letter size should be large enough so that viewers in the last row can see the text clearly. The recommended letter sizes are a) 3 cm tall can be read up to 10 meters distance from the board b) 6 cm tall can be read up to 20 meters distance from the board c) The thickness of the letters should be $1/5^{th}$ of the height of the letter.
- Write slowly with even pressure on the chalk in a straight line.
- Don't speak while writing on the board.
- The lower edge of the chalkboard should be at the level of the viewers' eyes.
- The closest viewer should be about 3 meters from the chalkboard.
- No other teaching aid should be in front or beside thechalk board to avoid distraction.
- Always clean the chalkboard when starting a new subject. Advantages
- Step-by-step presentation of the topic creates a dramatic impact and sustains audience interest.
- A colourful effect may be produced by using coloured chalk.
- Presentations may be adjusted according to the receptivity of the audience.

- Helps the audience to take notes. 68 Extension Teaching Methods and Audio Visual Aids
- Helps in comprehension and retention of knowledge.
- Economic, simple to construct, use, and maintain. Limitations
- Bad handwriting of a extension worker may confuse the audience.
- The blackboard communication is temporary. 3.5.2 White Board Modern classrooms are equipped with boards, also called marker boards or multipurpose boards.

- They can be used for more than one purpose.
- They are dustless and hygienic.
- They are preferred around computers as dust can harm computers.
- They require special erasable markers.
- A felt eraser is required to erase the surface soon after use.
- Markers are available in different colours.

Purpose

- It can be used for the same purpose as a blackboard, with more clarity.
- A variety of colour markers can be used for effectiveness.
- It may be used as surface for projecting films, slides, and overhead transparencies.

White board

A white board with a steel backing can be used as magnetic board for display. 3.5.3 Bulletin Board A bulletin board displays message. It is a surface on which bulletins, news, information, announcements, of specific or general interest can be displayed. Bulletin boards are of different sizes with provisions to hold pins, books exhibits and other materials. A bulletin board may be covered with soft insulation or perforated masonite, and may or may not be covered with glass. Fixing, dismantling and re-fixing message is very convenient on both types of boards. The message on the bulletin board may be in the form of words, graphs, charts, photographs, illustrations, publications, etc.

Purpose

- To decorate the office with photographs, pictures or tastefully selected materials for the benefit of office visitors.
- To announce film shows, demonstrations, visits by extension workers.
- To remind people to get a inoculations, spray their houses, weed their crops.
- To make comparisons. Example: Photographs of well nourished and poorly nourished children Desirable Features for Bulletin Boards
- Writing should be legible from a distance.
- The materials should be related with the objectives.
- A combination of facts, pictures drawing and other materials can add variety.
- Decorative materials, such as coloured papers, tapes, pins, etc., should be used to enhance the attractiveness of the board.
- Highlight the main theme with a catchy illustration, caption, or text, or it may be the brightest or largest item on the board.
- Simplicity and brevity are keys to good arrangements. In addition, timeliness, Audio-Visual Aids variety, continuity, order, colour, spacing and balance are important.
- Keep the bulletin board neat and clean; remove the old materials promptly when no longer required.

- Advantages
- Draws attention to important extension announcements.
- Facilitates the display of graphic and pictorial matter.

· Highlights current extension and development activities and achievements.

Pictures and Photographs

A picture is a representation made by drawing, painting, or photography which gives an accurate idea of an object. A good picture may tell a story without using a single word. Pictures may be in black and white, or in colour. Colour pictures and enlarged photographs have more appeal. For extension photography, a good quality 35 mm. single-lens reflex camera with some essential attachments like a flash gun, lens hood, filters, close-up lens, etc. are useful. However, due to processing and preservation problems of negatives, as well as with the advancement of technology, now digital cameras are more popular.

Purpose/Uses Pictures and photographs are used in various ways in extension work such as

· training programmes,
· publication,
· campaign,
· exhibition,
· slide,
· filmstrip,
· motion picture,
· television,
· newspaper and display etc.
· Photographs pasted with synthetic adhesive on thick board and cut to shape by ferret machine can produce good display material with 3 -dimensional effect.

Rope Board

Rope, wire, heavy string can be used to create a background for pictures or exhibit materials. The rope can be stretched from floor to ceiling. Pictures mounted on cardboard or three dimensional objects can be taped in place. A heavy wire screen can also be used as a background.

Flannel Board and Flannel Graph

A flannel board is a visual aid in which messages are written or drawn on thick paper and presented step-by-step by the extension worker to the audience to synchronize with the talk. The board is a flannel covered flat surface. Flannel is stretched and then glued to a piece of plywood or heavy cardboard. The name of the board comes from the kind of cloth that coveres it:

· Flannel board- If covered with flannel cloth.
· Felt board – If covered with felt cloth.
· Khaddar board – If covered with khadi cloth, and so on.

Flannel Graph

Graphic materials like cut-out pictures, photographs writing on a piece of paper and backed by sand paper or flannel cloth are known as flannel graphs. When these flannel graphs are placed on a flannel board, they stick to the surface. Under field conditions, a rough cloth, a bed sheet,/ old blanket, khaddar, or flannel can be spread on any flat surface such as a chalk board, which also works like a flannel board. By pasting strips either of flannel or sandpaper to the backs of pictures, or to other instructional material, they can be made to cling to the flannel board. Purpose The appeal of a flannel board demonstration is that a progressive story can be unfolded before the learner's eyes. The action of the moving parts attracts attention and stimulates interest. It can be of particular interest to illiterates for telling many kinds of educational stories. Clever extension workers can place interesting pieces on the board, and keep the audience wondering how the story will end, until the final piece is placed. Its capacity for building up suspense is the chief advantage in using a flannel board or flannel graph.

Preparation

- The board should be at least 30 × 40 inches and much larger if needed. 71 · Flannel must be light in colour for most uses – light grey, light tan, or green Audio-Visual Aids are good colours for the purpose.
- If the board is to be carried about, it should be cut into two and hinged at the centre.
- Lean the board back slightly when in use so that materials stick easily to the board and are less likely to fall.
- The title of the story should be in large letters at the top of the board.
- The story materials can be drawings, photographs, or printed illustrations with sequence numbers.
- Keep the story simple.
- Use large and bold illustrations. Advantages
- Facilitate presentation of the talk as important points are already noted.
- Helps in clarifying concepts.
- Helps in showing the cumulative process.
- Produces a dramatic effect on the audience.
- Helps in summarizing the talk.
- Saves time in the presentation of a talk.

Limitations

- Suitable for a small group.
- Requires some preparation and practice. 3.5.7 Flash Cards Flash cards are brief visual messages on poster board cards flashed (turned over at short intervals) before the audience to emphasize important points in a presentation. Flash cards are held like a pack of cards and are flashed to the audience, one at a time, in a sequence, along with the talk.

Preparation

- A simple flash card is prepared by writing, printing or drawing on a plain sheet of white paper and pasting it to the cardboard.
- Limit the number of flashcards to 10 – 12.
- The size of the flash card should be: o 22"×28" for the group of 30 – 50 audience o 11"× 14" for small group.
- Letter size should be at least 1".
- Finish with a line drawing, or a cartoon.
- Brief notes about the contents of the first card should be written on the back of the last card; notes about the second card should be on the back of 1ˢᵗ card; notes about the third card should be on the back of second card, and, so on, till the end of all the cards.

Presentation

- The complete story and parts of the story on each card should be familiar to the presenter.
- Stack the cards in their proper order.
- Hold the card with one hand close to the chest against the body if the cards are small. If they are large, they may be placed on a high table. In any case, display the cards so that people can see them clearly.
- Flash the card in time along with the notes. For notes on the first card, you may quietly look at the notes written on the back side of the last card, and continue the sequence till the end.
- Slip the front card to the back of the set to change the card, or to illustrate the new point.
- Expose the card long enough for comprehension, or a glance.
- After the story is completed, display the cards on a bulletin board, or pass them on to the audience for glance.

- Use other teaching tools for comprehension. Advantages
- Can be made easily and quickly.
- Very simple to use and carry.
- Helps the speaker to emphasize the main points using the notes on the back of the cards.

Poster A

poster is displayed in a public place with the purpose of creating awareness amongst the people. A poster is generally seen from a distance and the person glancing at it seldom has the time or inclination to stop and read. The job of the poster is to stop the persons hurrying past, thrust the message upon them. A poster may contain a written message, diagram, map, picture, or a cartoon. A few hand drawn posters may be used in extension training programme, group meeting, etc. Printed posters may be used in large numbers in campaigns, exhibitions, etc.

Purpose

- Audio-Visual Aids The purpose of poster is to make a public announcement of a special idea with a few words and an illustration.
- A good poster is expected to take the learners through the first two steps in extension teaching, i.e., attention and interest.
- It is not expected to educate, but to stimulate action – either immediately or eventually.
- This requires a forceful idea, strongly presented by the content of the poster.
- It must be always a part of other teaching methods, viz., campaigns, meetings,

Preparation

- While preparing posters consider the following points.
- Promote a single idea or message.
- Must be timely.
- Follow ABC principle – Attractive, Brevity, and Clarity.
- It must be able to attract attention. the persons hurrying past must be stopped by some attractive feature in the poster to take a look at it. The design and use of a poster as a visual aid in extension teaching is based on this principle.
- It must be brief enough to convey the message clearly. The wording must be brief and illustrations easily understood, so that the message of the poster is quickly absorbed.
- Use simple colours – not more than three.
- Must be large enough to be seen easily – 22" × 28", 28"× 44", etc.

Advantages

- Helps in making announcements.
- Facilitates the display of ideas to the audience.

- Extension Teaching Methods and Audio Visual Aids
- Quick communication of a message to a large number of people.
- Easy to prepare and present.
- Highly economical.
- Highly versatile in use. Limitations
- Posters give only an initial idea and cannot furnish detailed information. They need to be supported for further information by another aid or method, e.g., leaflets and demonstration.
- The production of good posters is technical job and requires skill and time.

- Cannot be repeated – for each occasion a new poster has to be made. Note: Remove the poster after the programme, or when they have served their purpose.

Charts A

chart is a symbolized visual aid with pictures of relationships and changes used to tabulate a large mass of information, or show a progression.

Purpose

- Charts can help communicate difficult, often dull subject matter in an interesting and effective way.
- They make facts and figures clear and interesting, show or compare changes, show the size and placement of parts.
- They are also helpful in summarizing information and presenting abstract ideas in visual form.

Types of Charts

There are many varieties of charts. Some common types of charts are briefly discussed below for your understanding.

- **Bar Chart:** Bar charts are made of a series of bars along a measured scale. They are used to compare quantities at different times, or, under different circumstances.
- **Pie Chart:** Pie charts are in the shape of circles, and are used to show proportions and percentages.
- **Tabular chart:** Tabular charts are used to bring together mass related data in compact form. Example: timetable.
- **Tree chart:** Tree charts are used for showing development or growth of a programme or project. The origin is shown in a single line, or as a tree trunk, and various developments are shown as branches.
- **Flow Chart:** Flow charts show organizational structure of departments, institutions, resources with lines and arrows.
- **Pictorial Chart:** A pictorial chart gives the viewer a vivid picture, and creates a rapid association with the use of graphic messages, such as cartoons, and illustrations. Each visualized symbol indicates quantities. This type of chart is more useful for illiterate audience in extension work.
- **Overlay Chart:** Overlay charts consist of a number of sheets which can be placed, one over the other, conveniently. On each individual sheet a part of 75 Audio-Visual Aids the whole is drawn. This enables the viewer to see not only the different parts, but also how they appear when one is placed over the other. After the final overlay is placed, it shows the full view of the whole picture. This type of chart presentation is dramatic and effective.
- **Pull Chart:** A pull chart consists of written messages on a large sheet. Messages are hidden by strips of thick paper held in position by the slits provided on either side. The messages can be shown to the viewer one after another, by pulling out the concealing strips. The same strip can be replaced in the slits after showing the message. This type of chart presentation is dramatic and creates suspense for the viewer.
- **Strip Tease Chart:** They are similar to the pull chart, however, messages are concealed by strips of thin paper instead of thick paper. The ends of thin paper strips are pinned or pasted at both ends of the message. Whenever the message is to be exposed, one end of paper strip is stripped off. This has the advantage of surprise and anticipation.
- **Flip Chart:** A flip chart is a series of visuals drawn into large sheets of paper or cardboard, fastened together at the top. These are turned over or flipped, one at a time by the extension worker. This kind of chart exposes the audience to segments of the subject in sequence, and holds attention remarkably well.
- **Window Chart:** In this, flaps cover the messages and when the message is to be shown, the presenter open the flaps like windows. It creates suspense in the audience.

Preparation :

While preparing any type of chart, consider the following points.

- Keep it simple.
- Promote a single idea or message with important details.
- Maintain logical order.
- Use symbols, words, or colours to explain the chart.
- Use lines and bars in only one dimension.
- Compare units and avoid comparing unrelated units.
- The chart title must emphasize certain parts of diagrams. The title for 8"x 10½" sheet should be about ½" height, and for 30" x 40" charts, the height should be about 2½".

PROJECTED VISUAL AIDS

Any visual aid which is used for magnification of image on a screen in dark or semi-dark conditions can be called a projected visual aid. There are three important methods of projection:

- Direct projection - slide and film projectors
- Indirect projection – overhead projector
- Reflected projection – opaque projector, epidioscope.

Advantages Audio-Visual Aids

- Very effective aids to classroom teaching with a characteristic appeal of their own for influencing learners.
- When combined with audio aids or on the spot commentary, they prove to be very useful. Limitations
- Require special equipment for display.
- The equipment is costly, needs meticulous care and training for operation.
- Electricity/backup power is required for operation.
- The transportation and storage of equipment needs special attention.
- The quality of projection depends on the kind of screen, placement of the audience in relation to the screen, and, the size of the image, and its brightness. However, the above limitations don't lessen the importance of using these visuals wherever suitable, due to their specific and definite advantages in extension and development work.

1 Slides

A slide is a transparent mounted picture which is projected by focusing light through it. The projection may be made on a screen or on a white wall. Slides of 35mm films, mounted on individual cardboard or plastic frames are common, and are extensively used in extension work during training programmes, seminars, workshops, group meetings, campaigns, exhibitions, etc.

2 . Overhead Projector

The overhead projector projects the picture over the head of the speaker on the screen. Drawings, diagrams, letterings, etc., are made on transparent sheets and are put on the glass platform of the overhead projector, through which a strong light is passed. The rays of light are made to converge with a lens, and are reflected by a mirror held at an angle on the screen at the back. The instructional items may be written or drawn by hand on transparent sheets, transparent cellophane, or polythene rolls with a special marker pen, in colour or in black and white. Transparencies can also be made through photographic, xerox, or electronic processes as well. Overhead projection is used in training programmes, group meeting, seminar, symposium, workshop, etc.

Advantages

- Projection may be synchronized with the talk by facing the audience and observing their reaction.
- The presenter can also write, make sketches, and erase while projecting.
- Covering a portion of the transparency with a sheet of paper and making progressive disclosure, and superimposing diagrams may be achieved effectively.

- Makes the talk dynamic and sustains audience interest.
- Complex ideas may be clearly presented.
- Saves time in presenting the talk.
- Easy to prepare and project the instructional materials.
- Materials for transparencies are cheap and easily available.

3 Handheld Projector

The handheld projector is also known as a pocket projector, or a mobile projector, or a pico- projector. It is an emerging technology that applies the use of a projector in a handheld device. It is a response to the emergence of compact portable devices such as mobile phones, personal digital assistants and digital cameras, which have sufficient storage capacity to handle presentation materials with an attached display screen. Handheld projectors involve miniaturized hardware and software that can project digital images on to any nearby viewing surface, such as a wall or screen. A handheld projector has the ability to project a clear image, regardless of the physical characteristics of the viewing surface.

Audio Visual Aids

Audio visual aids are those devices through which messages can be seen as well as heard, simultaneously. Synchronization of these two important senses leads to more learning and more retention when compared to the use of visual and audio senses separately. We learnt from the previous section that the two senses, sight and hearing, together, attracts 94 % of audience attention. This is clear cut evidence that audio visual aids can play an important role in extension teaching.

Advantages

- Convey meaning clearly in a condensed form and clarify ideas better.
- Supplement spoken word.
- Supply a concrete basis for conceptual thinking.
- Attract the attention, arouse, as well as sustain, the interest of the audience.
- Make learning more permanent.
- Overcome limitations of space, time, and distance.
- Develop continuity of thought with motion pictures.
- Stimulate self activity, and motivate people for action.

1 Motion Pictures

Motion pictures are extremely useful in motivating and teaching any learner. Yet educational films are not being widely used by extension educators in many development sub sectors. The reasons usually given are:
- The expense of films and projectors.
- Non availability of suitable films.
- Transportation and maintenance of films and projectors.
- Dominance of entertainment over educative function of films.
- Lack of skills, on the part of extension workers, to operate projectors. Seating Arrangements for a Motion Picture Show The farthest seat from the screen should not be more than 6 times the width of the picture on the screen. Don't seat learners closer to the screen than twice the width of the picture. With a canvas/matte screen, the viewing angle should not exceed 300, and with a beaded screen the angle should not exceed 250. The bottom of the screen should be about one foot above the heads of the audience.

Preparation

- See the preview of the educational film and assure yourself that it is suitable for the planned extension activity and intended audience.
- Note down important teaching points and difficult words that audience might not understand.

- Compose a few questions which are answered in the film.
- Make sure that the projector and film are in good condition and that there is sufficient darkness in the presentation area, before the arrival of the audience.

Presentation

- Make your audience aware that the purpose of the film is educational and not entertainment, and that they will be expected to learn the messages from it.
- Tell them the title of the film and say, generally, what the film is about.
- Explain why this film is important and relate it to their own self interests.
- Write the questions that you composed on the chalkboard and inform them that these questions will be answered by the film.
- Try to show the film without any breaks or distractions.
- Immediately after film screening, encourage the audience to discuss it, freely.
- Distribute relevant literature, and provide contact addresses for further information.
- Demonstrate the skill, if any, showed in the film.
- If required show the film again. Advantages
- Combines sound and sight, acting on two senses at the same time.
- Attracts and holds attention due to illuminated screen in semidarkness.
- Overcomes the barrier of illiteracy – it communicates extension ideas to anyone who can see and hear.
- Audiences identify themselves with the story on the screen, thus producing highly emotional responses.
- Brings audiences closer to the objects, places, and situations that they cannot ordinarily see in their daily lives.

Limitations
· Requires a lot of planning and preparation on part of extension workers.
· The audiences' focus may be on entertainment rather than education.
· With the advent of television, video, and digital technology, the importance of motion pictures has been reduced.

Video Projector

A video projector is also known as a Digital Projector, now popular for many applications for extension and development. All video projectors use a very bright light to project the image. Projected image size is important because the total amount of light does not change - as size increases, brightness decreases. They are widely used with, or without a connection to an interactive white board for presentations, training, demonstrations, etc. CRT projector that uses cathode ray tubes is the oldest system still in regular use, but falling out of favour largely because of the bulky cabinet. An LCD projector using LCD light gates is the simplest system, making it one of the most common and affordable, currently.

Interactive White Board

An interactive white board is a large interactive display that connects to a computer and projector. A projector projects the computer's desktop onto the board's surface, where users control the computer using a pen, finger, or other device. The board is typically mounted to a wall, or on a floor stand.

Purpose

· It is a replacement for a whiteboard, flipchart, or video, or, othern media system, such as a DVD player and TV combination.

· Can interact with online information from anywhere.

· Captures notes written on the whiteboard for later distribution.

· Some interactive whiteboards allow recording the instruction as digital video files for review – a very effective instructional strategy for learners who benefit from repetition, for those who need to see the material presented again, those who are absent, for struggling learners, and, for future review.

· With its integrated audience response system, presenters can get feedback.

· Helps to teach abstract, difficult concepts and complex ideas – visual tools help learners concentrate for longer and understand more fully.

· Technology has the capability of bringing lessons to life and making the lessons much more enjoyable for the learner. Limitations

· Can be useful in the classroom situation with advanced facilities, but not under field conditions.

· Permanent markers, for example, can create problems on some interactive whiteboard surfaces. (Punctures, dents and other damage to surfaces are a risk, but do not typically occur in the normal course of classroom use).

· The technology was initially welcomed by learners, however, it seems that any boost in their motivation is short-lived.

· It is possible that learners focus more on the new technology rather than on what they should be learning.

· In lower ability groups, it could actually slow the pace of learning of the whole class, as individual learners take turns at the board.

Multimedia and Multiple Media

Multimedia is a combination of more than one media, but it could include several forms of media audio, text, still images, animation, graphics, video, and film. The use of more than one aid is increasingly common. Even earlier, multiple media presentations were assembled with the available traditional audio visual aids resources.

Example: Combinations of overhead projectors, flipcharts and slide projectors. Multimedia in a more current context generally implies a computer based media. The term, computer based multimedia, has become very popular. Interactive video is one form of computer based multimedia. With computer based multimedia, information access is simplified. Sophisticated databases can organize vast amounts of information which can be quickly sorted, searched, found, and cross indexed.

Example: Through information kiosks, a lot of developmental information is being accessed in remote and rural areas. The advantage of using multiple media is that it can greatly increase the impact of presentation. It can also lead to a confused presentation, if not planned very carefully. The best advice is to use multiple media only if needed.

KEYWORDS

Audio Aids : instructional devices through which message can only be heard. Visual Aids : instructional devices through which message can only be seen.

Audio Visual Aids : instructional devices in which the message can be heard and seen simultaneously.

Non projected Aids : visual instructional devices which are simply presented without any projection equipment.

Projected Aids : visual instructional devices which are projected and magnified by focusing light.

Display Aids Audio-Visual Aids : visual aids which are spread before the audience for viewing, who get the message by looking at them.

Presentation Aids : visuals aids, presented or projected before the audience for viewing, which explain, or present the message of the visuals, so that the audience understands of them.

Chalkboard/ Blackboard : probably the simplest, cheapest, most convenient, and widely used non projected visual aid in extension teaching.

White Board : modern class rooms are equipped with white boards which are also called as marker boards, or multi-purpose boards.

Bulletin Board : a board for displaying messages.

Flannel Board : a visual aid in which messages are written or drawn on thick paper and presented step-by-step by the extension agent to the audience and are synchronized with the talk.

Flash Cards : brief visual messages on poster board cards flashed (turned over at short intervals) before the audience to emphasize important points in a presentation.

Poster : a printed message displayed in a public place with the purpose of creating awareness amongst the people.

Charts : a symbolized visual aid with pictures of relationships and changes used to tabulate a large mass of information, or to show a progression.

Multimedia : a combination of more than one media, but it could include several forms of media and audio, text, still images, animation, graphics, video, and film.

<h1 style="text-align:center">VIII</h1>

Assessment

Assessment

Throughout the learning process, the teacher needs to track how well students understand the different subject matters being discussed. Educational assessments are one of the different methods and approaches that help the teacher realize this. It is an important part of learning and it provides useful feedback that improves pedagogy.

Educational assessment goes beyond standard end-of-term examinations and periodic tests. For instance, a teacher can ask students to create case studies as part of alternative assessments or use exit surveys to assess their knowledge as they learn. In this article, we will discuss different methods of educational assessment and show you how to conduct each of them using Formplus forms.

Educational Assessment

Also known as educational evaluation, educational assessment is the systematic process of finding out about a student's knowledge, experience, skills, and beliefs using empirical data. The ultimate goal is to quantify and document how much a student knows.

There are different ways to carry out educational assessments. For instance, you can ask students to write an exam that tests their knowledge or to execute tasks that show how much they have learned. Education assessment is a continuous process and the results help you improve teaching and learning experiences in the classroom.

Educational evaluation can happen both online and offline. During this process, the teacher or evaluator can pay attention to one student at a time. They can also choose to consider the students as a group or assess the entire learning community at a go.

Types of Educational Assessment

Alternative Assessment

Alternative assessment is an evaluation method that measures a student's ability based on how they use newly-acquired knowledge to execute tasks. It is an instructor-led method of assessment that is specifically tailored to the needs and abilities of each student.

Instead of asking students to take part in standardized tests and quizzes, the instructor gets them involved in complex tasks where they need to leverage what they have learned. Alternative assessment methods help the teacher to have a full grasp of the student's level of proficiency in a subject.

To get the best results from alternative assessments, you need to align your methods with the overall goals and objectives of the training or subject. Common alternative assessment methods include asking students to create concept maps, write reports or partake in collaborative testing.

Advantages of Alternative Assessment

1. Alternative assessment methods objectively align with expected learning outcomes.
2. It pays attention to the quality of work from the students.

Disadvantages of Alternative Assessment

1. It can be time-consuming.

Examples of Alternative Assessment

What methods of alternative assessment should you try out in class? There are a number of choices you can explore however, your final decision should be in line with the unique learning needs of every student and your teaching goals. Here, we will discuss a few examples of alternative assessments.

- **Portfolio**

You can ask students to build out a portfolio that demonstrates their knowledge of what has been taught in a class or training. A portfolio is a collection of the different tasks a student has executed in the course of the class or training.

If you're handling learners in beginner classes, you can ask them to create a paper portfolio using a notebook; for advanced learners, an online portfolio is the best bet. You can create a simple submission form on Formplus to collect links to your students' portfolios easily.

- **Performance Test**

Since alternative assessment is all about putting knowledge to work, design effective performance tests to help you rate a student's level of skill or knowledge. A performance test requires the learners to execute complex tasks while the instructor observes how they go about them.

As an instructor, you should have well-defined scoring criteria to effectively measure each student's ability and arrive at a valid conclusion. Depending on the type of performance test you choose to adopt, you can create a quiz on Formplus for this purpose.

- **Open Tests**

An open test is a method of assessment that allows learners to refer to course materials as they take on tasks or write tests and examinations. The questions in an open test require the student to provide responses that show how well they understand the course.

Instead of memorizing the content of the training guide or course materials, the student has to apply the knowledge in the material(s) to provide the best response to the stated questions.

- **Crib Sheet**

This is another form of open-book evaluation. Instead of bringing the entire course materials to a test or examination, the student selects important information from these materials to create some sort of abridged version called the crib sheet.

While it's up to the student to decide what makes it into the crib sheet, you should provide some level of guidance as their instructor. You can subtly suggest the type of information that will be helpful during the assessment but you should not impose your ideas on the students; if you really want to know how much they know.

· **Take-Home Assessment**

Another way to assess your students' abilities is to give them take-home exercises. Take-home exercises typically check 2 boxes. Firstly, they require multiple references, and secondly, there isn't enough time for learners to do them in class.

· **Collaborative Testing**

This happens when you put the students in groups and get them to work together on different tasks. Ideally, you should pair them or place the students in small groups of 3 or 4, to get the best results from this exercise.

As the name suggests, collaborative testing empowers the students to brainstorm together, solve challenges, and execute ideas. At the end of each brainstorming session, you can ask your students to make individual submissions or submit collective responses as a group.

· **Summaries**

Instead of making students go through tests and assignments, you can ask them to summarise class readings, lectures, and discussions. A good summary tells you 1 thing—the student has an impressive understanding of key concepts and ideas from the classroom.

· **Reports**

Reports work just like summaries; they require the student to show how well they understand key concepts from class discussions. However, reports take things a step further as the student needs to communicate his or her knowledge in a way that presents a clear picture to whoever reads the report; even if such a person wasn't part of the class.

· **Interviews**

Pair students and ask them to perform interviews about different subject matters discussed in your class. For instance, if you had a class discussion on a historical event, one student can roleplay as a key event player while the other person becomes the interviewer; asking questions about that event.

· **Concept Maps**

Aconcept map is a visual representation of the relationship between ideas and concepts. To test your students' level of understanding, ask them to build concept maps from scratch to show their knowledge or fill out existing concept maps.

Authentic Assessment

This is a realistic method of evaluation that places students in complex, real-life situations and asks them to use their knowledge to resolve them. As students put their knowledge to work, they gain a clearer understanding of the course content and subject matter.

Unlike traditional assessment methods that focus just on the students' performance, authentic assessment is all about using one's knowledge to solve real-life tasks. Students find authentic assessments more interesting because they involve real-life contexts they can relate to.

Authentic assessment is a two-way street. On one hand, it helps students to improve their skills and on the other hand, it evaluates how much a student knows in real-life contexts. As part of authentic assessment, students may be asked to develop a business plan for an existing organization or troubleshoot a problem.

Advantages of Authentic Assessment

1. It converts students into active participants in the educational evaluation process.
2. While helping students to become better learners, it also empowers the instructors to be better teachers.

Disadvantages of Authentic Assessment

1. It is highly subjective and this makes it difficult to grade students using authentic assessment methods.
2. Authentic assessments typically require detailed, personalized, and specific feedback which can take a lot of time; especially when you have a large class.

Characteristics of Authentic Assessment

1. Authentic assessment simulates real-life situations. Students are asked to participate in real-world tasks and activities to demonstrate their knowledge of the course or subject matter.
2. There are no right or wrong answers in authentic assessment. It is all about showing how the student can use the knowledge from the course in real-world contexts and scenarios.
3. Authentic assessment questions are presented as poorly-structured problems.
4. It requires in-depth creativity and originality. The students have to think outside the box to create unique solutions to the problem.
5. Authentic assessment methods are tailored to 1 specific and well-defined purpose.
6. It is complex and action-oriented. Alternative assessments spur the students to research and look for answers. The students need to leverage a variety of skills and data collection methods to find practical solutions.
7. Authentic assessment involves both oral tests like presentations and written tests with open-ended questions.
8. Students get feedback from the instructor at different points as they engage in the tasks. It allows the students to leverage feedback and improve their solutions and suggestions until they arrive at the most practical and effective answers.
9. The instructor collaborates with the students to create alternative assessments.

Examples of Authentic Assessment

- **Studio Portfolios**

This is a meaningful collection of student's performance and an in-depth evaluation of how they have put their knowledge to work. Studio portfolios show clear patterns of a student's growth and this helps the teacher to quantify the student's progress and performance. As students create their portfolios, they reflect on their goals and engage in some degree of self-assessment.

- **Role-Play**

This is a type of experiential learning where the student takes on a specific role or character in a well-defined learning context. Unlike simulation games, role play places students in distinct roles. The students may be asked to imitate characters in unfamiliar contexts.

- **Memos**

A memo relays information about a defined subject matter using the first-person point of view. Students collate data and then, use their imagination to weave texts from different perspectives. Sometimes, they can write like a real or imagined historical individual for a real or imagined audience.

- **Presentations**

Presentations are the most common method of authentic assessment. Students get to discuss their work and validate their ideas in the presence of a mixed audience made up of their classmates, teachers, and external stakeholders like parents and technocrats.

Presentations build up students' confidence and communication skills. Also, they prompt the students to take extra care and invest more time and thought before bringing their ideas forward. Since the students get to use different tools like slides and sticky notes for the presentation, they also develop some level of proficiency with these tools.

You need to guide the students as they prepare for their presentations. You can ask them to prepare and turn in their slides early for review. You may also organize a rehearsal to help them get comfortable with speaking to an audience.

- **Fishbowls**

A fishbowl is a special type of group discussion involving hot seats. The teacher selects a small group of students who sit on these "hot seats" and respond to questions, ideas, and suggestions from the rest of the class on a specific topic or subject matter.

Think of a fishbowl as a panel session with students acting as both panelists and members of the audience. The members of the audience sit in a circular arrangement around the panelists to map out the perimeter of the fishbowl.

Fishbowls are not impromptu; the students are given the topic of discussion ahead of time, and this allows them to prepare adequately. Apart from testing the students' knowledge of the subject matter, fishbowls also improve communication, active listening, comprehension, and group discussion skills.

- **Simulation Games**

Sometimes, the teacher creates a case study with different scenarios mirroring the specific topic or subject matter discussed in the class. Students are then assigned different roles within the case study or asked to play different characters within the scenarios.

The students get copies of the case study before the simulation game. This way, they fully internalize their roles and have access to data, background information, and the descriptions of the characters they will represent in the game.

Mock court proceedings, mock doctor-patient consultations, and simulated town hall meetings are common examples of simulation games that happen in the classroom.

- **Case Studies**

You can ask your students to build up case studies of real-life contexts related to the subject matter. For instance, in gender and reproductive health training, students may conduct an in-depth evaluation of maternal mortality rates in their community, and present their findings.

A lot of work goes into building case studies. The students have to draft different closed-ended and open-ended research questions and collect real-time data from members of the research population using different methods including surveys, interviews, and observation.

- **Proposals**

A proposal is a well-researched document that shows how a student will solve a particular problem. Here, the student needs to outline his or her ideas, tie these ideas to specific goals and objectives, and justify the methods to be used for solving the problem.

Writing a proposal is important because it allows students to vet their ideas and develop a full-proof solution. It is a blueprint for the student's final project and it convinces the instructor to approve the ideas and suggestions for further exploration.

To collect submissions easily from students, you can create a simple online submission form with Formplus. This form has a file upload field where students can submit e-copies of their proposals. It also has several text fields where students can fill in project descriptions and their bio-data.

- **Policy Briefs**

A policy brief is a formal, structured, and professional presentation of a proposal. It is written in industry jargon for a specialized target audience who already know about the problem and may have even carried out some level of research on the subject matter.

In many cases, the student is asked to present the policy brief during a seminar or other similar academic events. For example, students in Applied Linguistics can write a policy brief on instrumental phonetics, and students of Counselling can present a policy brief on juvenile delinquency.

- **Reports**

Students may observe real-life contexts related to a particular subject matter and submit a report on their observations within a specific period. For example, after volunteering in a local charity event, students can complete an online report sheet or turn in their reports via a Formplus online submission form.

Summative Assessment

Summative evaluation is the most common method of classroom assessment. This method of evaluation involves using a standard or rubric to grade a students' performance at the end of a training course, or program.

In summative assessment, the instructor compares what the student knows with what was taught, and uses the result to determine whether they move to the next level of a course. Summative evaluation monitors the student's performance against expected learning outcomes.

Validity, reliability, and practicality are the most common features of summative assessment. Examples of summative assessment include end-of-term examinations, standardized tests, and creative portfolios. These high-stake methods produce results that define a learner's progress.

Advantages of Summative Assessment

1. It is a standardized method of assessment.
2. Summative assessment plays an important role in moving students from one level to another.

Disadvantages of Summative Assessment

1. It can discourage students; especially when the results do not turn out to be what they want.

Characteristics of Summative Assessment

- **Validity**

Summative assessment measures a student's competence in a specific subject matter in line with the learning goals and objectives of the course or training. For instance, a science course will use experiments and other practical tests to evaluate a student's knowledge at the end of the course.

- **Reliability**

Summative evaluation is a standardized method of knowledge-based assessments. It has well-defined processes that reveal the student's competence in a field. These processes produce accurate and consistent results when they are used in similar contexts.

- **Practicality**

Summative evaluation has a flexible process that is practical and scalable. It is well-aligned and this makes it easy for the instructor to implement it as part of a training.

- **Ethical**

Summative assessment respects clear teaching and learning boundaries. Before the instructor implements any summative assessment methods in the classroom, he/she must obtain informed consent from the students.

- **Easily reported**

Since the key element of summative assessment is to evaluate what someone has learned up to that point in time, it always ends in having a concise summary of the outcomes of the assessment. This allows the teacher to compare the student's current performance with past performances, external standards, and other learners.

- **Variety**

Summative evaluation prompts students to exhibit skills and demonstrate knowledge in different ways.
Other things you should have in mind when it comes to summative assessment are:

1. It takes place at the end of a defined learning period such as a training or program.
2. It is limited to the information that was shared during the course or training. Summative assessment does not test students on what they have not been taught.
3. Summative assessment aligns with the learning goals and objectives of the course.
4. Summative assessment certifies a student's competence in a specific subject matter.
5. It is used for one clearly identified purpose.

Examples of Summative Assessment

- **End-of-term Examination**

A final examination or assessment is one of the most common methods of classroom evaluation. Examinations have a simple framework—the teacher curates relevant questions and the students respond to these questions within a timeframe.

Instructors conduct examinations as some sort of final knowledge review of the program. Examinations test the students' knowledge of the subject matter and they produce quantitative results that help you to grade your students and know how well they have performed.

To eliminate the workload that comes with paper assessment, you conduct the evaluation via an online test platform, examination software, or create a quiz on Formplus. The examination questions can be close-ended, open-ended, or a mixture of both; depending on the type of data you want to gather in the end.

- **In-class Chapter Tests**

These are mini-examinations that happen at the end of a topic or section of training. They are used to determine how well a student understands key chapter concepts and help them prepare for the final examination at the end of the course. Quizzes, midterm assessments, and practice tests are common examples of chapter tests.

- **Standardized Admission Tests**

These tests qualify candidates for a specific program; for instance, IELTS and TOEFL are standardized English-proficiency exams that demonstrate a candidate's competency in the use of the language. These tests are organized on a large scale and they make use of explicit scoring criteria for grading.

- **Creative Portfolio**

Instead of an end-of-term examination, ask students to build a creative portfolio. A creative portfolio showcases the student's creativity, knowledge of the coursework, and how they have uniquely applied that knowledge.

Depending on the learning areas, a student's portfolio can include images, infographics, and small to medium-length texts like essays or one-pagers. As the learners build their portfolios, they also have the opportunity to reflect on how much they have learned.

Add the file upload field to your Formplus form to receive portfolio submissions from your students. Students can submit files of any type and size including images, multiple document formats, and spreadsheets, in the file upload field.

- **Oral Tests**

Oral summative assessments are used to get real-time and spontaneous responses from learners at the end of a course. The instructor can embrace structured, semi-structured, or unstructured interview methods to grade the students and evaluate their overall performance. Students may also partake in oral classroom presentations.

The type of interview method you choose determines the kinds of questions you will ask during the process. A structured interview follows a defined conversational sequence that dictates its questions and structure.

Semi-structured and unstructured interviews embrace flexibility. In a semi-structured interview, the instructor can veer off the conversational sequence and ask spontaneous questions. Unstructured interviews do not follow a defined conversational sequence—the instructor can ask questions as they come, within the course's context.

- **Hands-on Performance Tasks**

These simple and creative tasks allow students to put their knowledge to work. Hands-on performance tasks are practical, straightforward and help the instructor to assess the students' abilities directly.

The instructor can ask students to solve a jigsaw puzzle and as they do this, she observes how they put a specific skill to work in the tasks. If you want to assess your students' counting and pattern skills, you may observe how they play around with colored bricks or cotton balls.

- **Group Projects**

Getting students to execute tasks within small groups is a great way to test their knowledge. After a training on teamwork and conflict resolution, for instance, you should group the students, assign a task and watch how they create frameworks and solve a specific problem.

Formative Assessment

Formative assessment is an on-going educational evaluation method where the instructor assesses a student's knowledge during the learning process. It allows the instructor to keenly monitor learner's progress as they move from one learning phase to another. Formative assessment does not compare students' performance against some standard or rubric.

Because the teacher strictly monitors the student's performance, she can immediately recognize when the student starts struggling and step in to provide the right support. Formative assessment outcomes are non-graded and this means they do not produce results that define the learner's performance.

As part of formative assessment, the instructor can ask students to respond to quick-fire impromptu quizzes at the end of a lesson. Polls, entry and exit slips, interviews, and focus groups are other popular examples of formative assessment.

Advantages of Formative Assessment

1. Formative assessment empowers the instructors to make data-driven decisions.
2. It helps instructors to adjust their teaching methods to better suit the needs of the learners.

Disadvantages of Formative Assessment

1. Formative assessment can be time-consuming because the teacher needs to implement several methods to effectively monitor students' progress as they learn.
2. The more formative assessments you incorporate in the learning process, the lesser time there is for actual teaching.

Characteristics of Formative Assessment

Understanding the characteristics of formative assessment enables you to plan and execute one effectively as an instructor. For instance, knowing that formative assessment and learning happen concurrently will help you avoid waiting till the end of a course before evaluating your students.

Other things you should know about formative assessment include:

1. It evaluates the learning process and the learner's progress at the same time.
2. A formative assessment is collaborative as it measures the student's progress and the effectiveness of the teaching method.
3. Formative assessments are interwoven with the ongoing teaching and learning process.
4. It is a fluid method of evaluation. The student's progress is not measured against a standard or benchmark unlike what you will find with summative assessment methods.
5. Formative assessment requires the instructors and the students to become intentional learners.
6. The aim of formative assessment is to gather actionable feedback that improves the overall teaching and learning process.
7. It is a diagnostic method of evaluation.
8. Results from formative assessments are immediately made available.
9. Formative assessments are non-graded.

Examples of Formative Assessment

- **Impromptu Quiz**

After a lesson, you can ask students to take part in an impromptu quiz to know how well they understood the course material. An easy way to do this is by creating a short online quiz with relevant close-ended questions using Formplus.

- **Polls**

A poll is a way to gather instant feedback from students as they learn by asking the right questions. Formplus allows you to create simple and fun polls that help you to evaluate your students' knowledge as part of formative assessment.

With multiple form field options, you can have different types of rating questions in your poll including heart and emoji ratings. Formplus also has an automatic poll closing option; making it easier for you to integrate the online polls into the overall teaching and learning process.

- **One Minute Papers**

Another way to assess students' knowledge on the go is by asking them to create simple one-minute papers; they can do this online with Formplus. You can create a simple 1-minute survey with open-ended questions and ask your students to share their knowledge within a particular context.

- **Entry Slips**

Before starting off on a new topic or lesson, you can ask one or more questions to know how much the students remember from the previous lesson. You can edit any of our online surveys and list differentiated questions for the students to respond to.

- **Exit Slips**

Exit slips are used to measure the students' progress at the end of the lesson. Ask learners to write some of the points they remember from the lesson on scrap paper or create a simple online questionnaire on Formplus to collect relevant responses from students.

If you hosted the class on e-learning platforms like Google Classroom and Edulastic, you can track what your students know at a glance and also measure their progress, in line with the teaching and learning goals.

- **Dipsticks**

Think of these as easy and quick methods to know how well the learners understand different concepts discussed in class. You can ask learners to write short letters explaining core concepts to another person or do a think-pair-share exercise with a partner.

- **Visual Exercises**

Ask students to interpret core ideas from the course using simple visual representations. They can create basic sketches of what they have learned or you can create a simple survey and ask them to choose the most appropriate visual representation from the image options in your Formplus form.

- **Interviews and Focus Groups**

At specific intervals during the class, you can organize quick interviews and focus groups to assess the students. These can be in the form of casual discussions with the learners or 10-minutes structured interviews using an online survey or questionnaire. Organizing and focus groups can provide better contexts for the assessment.

- **Tag Feedback**

This is a peer assessment method where the students evaluate and provide feedback on each other's performance. As students assess their peers, you gain valuable insights into how well they understand the course material and topic(s).

Tag feedback is an effective way to get the students involved in formative assessment. Ask learners to highlight the positive contributions of their peers, or to suggest ways to improve the course content, teaching method, or overall classroom engagement.

- **Self-assessment**

One of the best ways to conduct formative assessments is to simply ask the students to do it themselves while you provide the needed guidance. When students evaluate themselves, they can reflect on their learning goals and discover their strengths and weaknesses.

High stakes Assessment

As the name suggests, high-stakes assessment is a method of evaluation that puts a lot of things on the line for the students. In other words, the results of high-stakes assessments are used to make important decisions about a learner's progress.

High-stakes assessments have consequences for learners. Passing these tests means significant progress for the student like getting promoted to the next class or receiving a new certificate. In the same way, failing these tests can prevent a learner from getting a certificate or earning a practice license.

Any method of evaluation that measures students' performance using some standard criteria is high-stakes. Because of the different consequences attached to a high-stakes test, students are motivated to give it their best shot and secure the best grades.

The difference between a high stakes assessment and low stakes assessment is functionality. While a low-stakes test would measure academic achievement, identify learning problems, or inform instructional adjustments, high-stakes assessments are used to score learning outcomes.

Summative assessment is a great example of high-stakes assessment.

Advantages of High Stakes Assessments

1. It creates a standard performance-evaluation and rating system.
2. It motivates students to put in their bests which helps to boost their performance.

Disadvantages of High Stakes Assessments

1. It puts students under a lot of pressure which harms their performance.
2. The results may not be a true reflection of the student's knowledge.

Pre-Assessment

Before students start a new course or training, the instructor can administer a short assessment to find out how much they already know about the topic. This process of evaluation is known as pre-assessment. With the pre-assessment results, the teacher can adjust the learning curriculum to meet the students' needs.

Pre-assessment should happen at every point where the student moves from one lesson to the other during the training or program. It allows the instructor to see things from the student's perspective and to adjust the course content to serve students effectively.

It also helps to prevent redundant learning. If you spend time repeating information that students already know, they can lose interest in the program, class, or training entirely. You'll also be wasting time that can be used for relevant knowledge impartation.

There are different ways to conduct pre-assessment during a program. For instance, you can ask students to share their thoughts about the new subject matter in a brief class discussion. Portfolio analysis, surveys, questionnaires, and concept maps are other ways to better understand what the learners already know.

Advantages of Pre-assessment

1. It allows you to see how much students know and what they can do before the course starts.
2. It communicates the course expectations to the students beforehand.

Disadvantages of Pre-assessment

1. Pre-assessments can eat deep into the actual instructional time and reduce the actual learning duration.
2. It generates large data sets that can be time-consuming to process.

Performance Assessment

Performance-based assessments ask students to show how much they have learned rather than providing responses that simply tell the instructor what they know. In many instances, instructors use this as an alternative to summative evaluation.

Performance assessments allow students to own the overall evaluation process and it transforms them into active participants. By allowing the students to demonstrate their knowledge, performance assessments boost critical thinking and sharpen the students' analytical skills, problem-solving abilities, and communication skills.

All authentic assessment methods are performance-based. Examples of tasks that allow students to demonstrate their knowledge include individual and group presentations, creative portfolios, journals and projects, and public speaking contests.

Advantages of Performance-based Assessment

1. It promotes active student engagement in the classroom.
2. It is a flexible and direct method of assessment.

Disadvantages of Performance-based Assessment

1. It relies on specific skill sets like creativity and public-speaking which some students may not be great at.
2. The results of performance-based assessments are highly subjective.

Portfolio-based Assessment

In a portfolio-based assessment, the instructor asks students to submit a portfolio that details how much they have learned and the different projects they have worked on during the course. The instructor goes on to assess this portfolio to grade the student's knowledge and performance.

A portfolio-based assessment allows students to show what they have learned outside the strict parameters of traditional assessment methods. You can create a simple online submission form to collect portfolio submissions as file uploads on Formplus.

Portfolio assessment enables students to focus on their real performance, and show their strengths and weaknesses. It makes it easy for the instructor to observe the student's progress during the learning process. More than this, as students create their portfolios, they can reflect on their learning experiences and self-evaluate their abilities and performance.

Advantages of Portfolio-based Assessment

1. It provides real-time feedback on students' growth and progress during the course.
2. It allows the teacher to assess individual talent.

Disadvantages of Portfolio-based Assessment

1. Grading portfolio-based assessment can be highly subjective.
2. It is time-consuming.

Diagnostic Assessment

A diagnostic assessment is a method of educational evaluation that instructors use to find out how much a student knows about a topic. It happens before a new training, course, or lesson, and it helps the teacher to kickstart teaching and learning on the right note.

Diagnostic assessments are quite similar to formative evaluation methods. However, the big difference is while formative assessment happens as learning takes place, diagnostic evaluation analyses what students have learned in the past. It sets the mood for learning by creating knowledge expectations.

Advantages of Diagnostic Evaluation

1. It gives the teacher a concise overview of how much the students know.
2. It creates an effective context that improves learning.

Disadvantages of Diagnostic Evaluation

1. It is time-consuming.
2. It may not provide a true reflection of the student's knowledge.

How to Use Formplus for Educational Assessment

All the methods of educational evaluation we have discussed so far involve gathering meaningful data from the students for assessment and sometimes, grading. To do this, you need a powerful tool that can help you create surveys, quizzes, and questionnaires to gather the information you need. Formplus is one of the best online platforms for this.

Formplus is a data-collection tool that supports online and offline data gathering. With Formplus, you can create different types of forms for educational evaluation. Here's how to use Formplus as an educational assessment tool.

Advantages of Educational Assessment

1. Educational assessment helps the instructor to track student's performance and progress before, during, and after learning.
2. In the case of formative assessment, the teacher gets immediate and effective feedback on the students' level of understanding and this empowers them to provide any required support.
3. Educational assessment allows you to create unique evaluation parameters that suit the needs and experiences of different learners.
4. It gives you a bird' eye view of the overall teaching and learning process.
5. Results from educational assessment go a long way to improve the learning curriculum and teaching methods in schools.
6. A well-designed educational assessment method converts students into active participants in the learning process. It empowers students to demonstrate their knowledge and conduct self-evaluation.
7. Educational assessment helps the teacher to know how well the students understand a specific concept or the entire course material.

Conclusion

As we've shown you in this article, there are various ways of conducting educational assessments; you only need to find the method that works best for you and your students. The best part is, you can use more than one educational evaluation method; for instance, combining formative and summative assessments, in a single learning process.

What are Multiple Choice Questions (MCQs)?

Multiple choice questions (MCQs) are a form of assessment for which students are asked to select one or more of the choices from a list of answers.

Structure of MCQs

MCQ consists of a stem and a set of options. The stem is usually the first part of the assessment that presents the question as a problem to be solved; the question can be an incomplete statement which requires to be completed and can include a graph, a picture or any other relevant information. The options are the possible answers that the student can choose from, with the correct answer called the key and the incorrect answers called distractors.

Advantages of MCQs

- Good MCQs are designed to be objective. They usually have one (or a few) definite answers that are given as choices for the students to select. Thus there will be no ambiguity in marking due to subjective factors in the questions. Objective MCQs are easy to mark (a set of answer sheets is all that is required from the assessor) and thus do not require experienced tutor to mark them.
- MCQs take less time to complete, with shorter assessment time required, more questions can be assessed. Feedback is fast.
- MCQs can be administered as on-line assessments, such online assessments can be very effective, and can prompt correct answers directly after completion with clarification and reasoning of the answers.
- Factors irrelevant to the assessed material (such as handwriting and clarity of presentation) do not come into play in multiple choice assessments. (Wikipedia accessed 13 Jun 08)
- MCQs have high reliability, validity and manageability.

Disadvantages of MCQs

- MCQs are typically used for assessing knowledge only, students may often memorize MCQs with rote learning. If assessors wish to use MCQs to assess deeper learning, careful attention (and many practices) on appropriate questions are required.
- MCQs are usually used as formative assessments during class. They have a reputation of being easy. Thus students tend to receive higher marks in comparison to other assessments such as essays, reports, and presentations etc., for which a "glass ceiling" of around the 80% mark are often incurred. Care must be taken to design MCQs which have the same level of difficulty as other assessments. Obviously, students are unlikely to complain if they receive high marks in a formative MCQ assessment, but for summative assessment, if a different assessment method is used (which is usually the case), then students should be given clear assessment procedures and expectations. It is advisable to give practices on other assessments if such assessments are used for summative assessment.
- Guessing – with MCQs there is a possibility of guessing the correct answer, there are numerous methods to penalize students from guessing, such as negative marking (not recommended as sometimes produce negative effects to students who know the answers), more options to answers, adopting mathematical strategies to normalise marks, giving partial marks to an answer very near the correct answer.
- MCQs cannot test oral or written skills, it can test only the theories.

How to design good MCQs?

1. When writing the stem, use clear and direct language. The stem should be able to clearly identify the question. Avoid complex wordings which may confuse and frustrate students with sound understanding.
2. Avoid using unnecessary and irrelevant material.
3. You are not trying to catch your student out, so try not to use negatives. If negatives are used, highlight, bold or italicize it.
4. Put as much of the question in the stem as possible, rather than duplicating material in each of the options.
5. Use only plausible and attractive alternatives as distractors.
6. Avoid giving clues to the correct answer.
7. If possible, avoid the choices "All of the above" and "None of the above". If you do include them, make sure that they appear as correct answers some of the time.
8. Do bear in mind what you are trying to test. They should be aligned with the intended learning outcomes.
9. Carefully designed questions will discourage rote learning.

Marking Rubrics

MCQs do not require any specific grading standards or criteria as the answers are usually set and defined. Thus as long as the assessors have a set of answer sheets with the correct choices marked, MCQs can be easily assessed and graded. Negative marking can also be administered (but not recommended). The following Grading scheme is often used for MCQs: (From WebCT)

- **Equally weighted:** This option will allocate an equal value to each answer. For example if the question is worth 20 points with four question and answer pairs, the student with two correct answers will be awarded 10 points and the student with 3 correct answer will get 15 points.
- **All or nothing:** The student must get all the matches correct for this question or they will receive a score of zero.
- **Right minus wrong:** The number of incorrect matches are subtracted from the correct matches to give the student a score. For example, in a question worth 30 points with three question and answer pairs, a student with two correct answers and one incorrect answer will be awarded ten points (20-10).

What is an Essay?

An Essay is an assessment question that requires an answer in a sentence, paragraph, or short composition. Essay assessments are usually classified as subjective assessments as there are normally a variety of responses.

Structure of Essay (Trigwell, K. (1992). Information for UTS Staff on Assessment)

According to Trigwell, there are 3 standard forms of essays:

1. **Role Play Essays**

   Students respond to the essay as if he/she is performing a specific role in the essay.

   For example: Write a letter to the local county council, explaining the environmental issues in the area, and requesting them to produce some measures; giving evidences and social arguments from government reports.

   This type of essays allows the students to become involved and see the relevance of the task.

2. **Structured Essays**

   Structured Essays are essays which have specific questions or topics that require answers.

   For example: In Shakespeareï¿½s play ï¿½ Hamlet, discuss and compare some of the soliloquies in terms of its style, syntax and imagery.

   This type of essays is useful if the assessors wish to test specific knowledge and techniques, it is also easier to mark as the assessors know what type of answers to expect.

3. **Interpretation of Data Evidence Essays**

   Students are asked to write an essay based on data from a report/experiment they produced or from an external source.

   For example: Using the measurements found in the laboratory, explain and discuss the chemical reactions between the two main elements found.

   This type of essays is greatly pragmatic, using data the students collected, allowing students to reflect and analyze.

An essay (depending on the types of essays) is usually expected to consist of an

1. Introduction/Aims/Objectives
2. Major points and ideas explained and summarized
3. Results/Related points/Issues/or others depending on the topic
4. Conclusion future work

Advantages of Essay Assessment

- Essays have the ability to assess all levels of learning objectives.
- It encourages original and creative thinking.

Disadvantages of Essay Assessment

- Due to the subjective nature of essay assessments, grading is very unreliable even for the same assessor at different periods.
- Grading may be influenced by other factors such as handwriting and length of response.
- As essays are very time-consuming to answer and to correct, they are not recommended if only low-level of learning outcomes are assessed which can be assessed by multiple choices or short answer questions.
- Although guessing is not possible in essay assessments, but ï¿½bluffingï¿½ is.
- It is also not advisable to give the topic of the essay to the students at an early date. This may give rise to superficial learning where students concentrate all their efforts in completing the essay only.

How to design a good Essay Assessment?

1. Let students know the assessment criteria and marking scheme, including grammar, spellings and other issues.
2. Try to reduce ambiguity in the essay questions, clearly define the expected response such as compare, evaluate, summarize, critique etc.
3. Do not use essays to measure knowledge or understanding that can be assessed using less time consuming assessment methods.

Marking Rubrics

There are two general grading approaches ï¿½ holistic and analytic grading. Holistic approach is grading the essay as a whole. Analytic approach grades the important components of the essay and assigns marks to each component.

MARKING RUBRICS

Excellent

Proficient

Average

Poor

CONTENT

Introduction:

Attitude is defined; thesis is clearly focused; subject is significant

Thesis is clear; provides direction for essay

Unclear; formulaic; not creative

Introduction is incomplete, ineffective, or missing

Idea Development:

Interesting; sophisticated; insightful

Clear and Thoughtful

Simplistic; uneven in quality; lacking in relevance

Absent or ineffective

Support or Evidence:

Detailed; accurate; convincing

Sufficient and accurate

Uneven

Vague, missing, or inaccurate

Word Choice:

Engaging and powerful choice of words

Appropriate to task

Uneven

Limited, monotonous, inappropriate

Conclusion:

Extends; connects; comments on topics

Purposeful and perceptive

Summarizes previously stated information

Absent, incomplete, or unfocused

ORGANIZATION

Topic Sentences:

Clearly related to thesis; comprehensive; incorporates effective transitions

Comprehensive and logical

Provides bland restatement of thesis; narrow or inaccurate

Absent

Paragraph Order:

Contributes to an effective argument; reinforces the content

Demonstrates a clear plan

Ineffective or inconsistent

Random

Transitions:

Effective and varied

Clear and functional

Mechanical

Absent

MECHANICS

Sentence Structure:

Complete; varied; interesting

Complete and correct

Variety is present; some errors are evident

Repetitious; fragments and run-ons are frequent

Punctuation/Spelling:

Error-free

Present but do not interfere with meaning

Careless or distracting

Block meaning

What are Objective Structured Clinical Examinations?

Objective Structured Clinical Examination (OSCE) was introduced by Harden and his colleagues in 1975. In an objective structured clinical assessment, a series of stations in an examination room is set up to examine students. At each station, students may be asked to carry out a procedure, which may involve taking history, performing preset clinical tasks and diagnosing patientsï¿½ problems. When performing the clinical tasks, students may often interact with ï¿½patientsï¿½, who may be healthy volunteers or mock patients. Students also have to answer questions based on their findings and their interpretation. Students are observed and scored at some stations by examiners with checklists.

Structure of Objective Structured Clinical Examinations

Objective Structured Clinical Examination consists of a series of stations that examines the competency of students in taking histories, practicing specific clinical tasks, and interpreting some clinical data. There are two types of stations in this assessment method:

1. **Practically-based** - Students are given a written instruction and have to carry out a procedure.

2. **Question-based** - Students have to answer questions on their findings at the previous station and interpret these findings. The questions may be open-ended or of multiple-choice type.

Students are assessed by examiners through a previously-determined, objective marking scheme. OSCE can be adapted into other disciplines such as science and engineering.

Advantages of Objective Structured Clinical Examinations

- Provides a uniform marking scheme for examiners and consistent examination scenarios for students.
- It provides an authentic way to assess medical students including pressure from patients.
- Generates formative feedback for both the learners and the teaching program. Immediate feedback collected may improve studentsï¿½ competency at subsequent stations and even enhance the quality of the learning experience.
- Minimizes the effect of cueing: When students go to a station, they will need to diagnose patientsï¿½ problems or carry out some clinical procedures. When they go to a subsequent station, they have to answer some questions relevant to their diagnosis or clinical tasks. However, students cannot go back to correct any mistakes or omissions on what they did in the previous station.
- More students can be examined at any one time. When a student is carrying out a procedure, another student who has already completed that stage is answering the question at another station.
- In the Objective Structured Clinical Examination, the setting is more controlled (only two variables exist: the patient and the examiner) and a more objective assessment of the student's clinical competency can be made.
- Provides more insights about studentsï¿½ clinical and interactive competencies.
- It can objectively assess other important aspects of clinical expertise, such as physical examination skills, interpersonal skills, technical skills, problem-solving abilities, decision-making abilities, and patient treatment skills

Disadvantages of Objective Structured Clinical Examinations

- It requires an extensive amount of organising.
- It is expensive in terms of manpower, resources and time (such as number of examiners, patients, and even space of examination room)
- It may discourage students from looking at the patient as a whole because the studentsï¿½ knowledge and skills are being put into compartments.
- The assessment examines a narrow range of knowledge and skills and does not test for history-taking competency properly. Students only examine a number of different patients in isolation at each station instead of comprehensively examining a single patient.

How to design a good Objective Structured Clinical Examination?
Steps in developing an Objective Structured Clinical Examination:

1. Decide the types of skills to be examined
2. Decide the types of assessment (such as a uniform checklist)
3. Consider the number of skill assessment stations needed (it is recommended to have 10 to 15 stations, and six minutes for each station) because the length of the examination is determined by the number of assessment stations and the time each candidate will spend at each station.
4. Allocate resources for the examination (such as space for examination rooms, marking sheets and plastic models)
5. Prepare the staff resources needed (including examiners, timekeepers and patient/volunteers)
6. Determine/arrange the day/period of exam
7. Conduct a review/evaluation of the arrangement of the exam after it is over

8. To design concise marking schemes that focus on actions that distinguish between good and poor performance
9. To provide marking scheme instructions on what students would do at each station for the examiners
10. To provide instructions which outline exactly the task required at each station for students

Marking Rubrics

Below is a sample of the OSCE rubric:

MARKING RUBRICS

Excellent

Proficient

Average

Poor

Diagnosis:

Able to give an excellent analysis and understanding on the patients' problems and situations and applied medical knowledge to the clinical practice and determined the appropriate treatment

Able to demonstrate medical knowledge with a satisfactory analysis on the patients' problems, and determined the appropriate treatment

Showed a basic analysis and knowledge on the patients' problems, still provided the appropriate treatment

Only able to show minimal level of analysis and knowledge on the patients' problems, unable to provide the appropriate treatment

Problem-solving skills:

Able to manage the time to suggest and bring out appropriate solutions to problems; more than one solutions were provided; logical approach to seek for solutions was observed

Able to manage the time to bring out only one solution; logical flow was still observed but there was a lack of relevance of the flow

Still able to bring out one solution on time; logical flow was hardly observed

Failed to bring out any solution in specific time; logical flow was not observed

Communication and interaction with patients:

Able to get detail information needed for diagnosis; gave very clear and detail explanation and answers to patients; paid attention to patients' responses and words

Able to get detail information needed for diagnosis; gave clear explanation and answers to patients; attempted but only paid some attention to patients' responses and words

Only able to get basic information needed for diagnosis; attempted to give a clear explanation to patients but omitted some points; did not pay attention to patients' responses and words

Failed to get information for diagnosis; gave ambiguous explanation to patients

Clinical skills:

Perfectly performed the appropriate clinical procedures for every clinical tasks with no omission; no unnecessary procedure was done

Performed the required clinical procedures satisfactorily; committed a few minor mistakes or unnecessary procedure which did not affect the overall completion of the procedure

Performed the clinical procedures at an acceptable standard; committed some mistakes and some unnecessary procedures were done

Failed to carry out the necessary clinical procedures; committed lots of mistakes and misconception about operating clinical apparatus

What are Short Answer Questions?

Short-answer questions are open-ended questions that require students to create an answer. They are commonly used in examinations to assess the basic knowledge and understanding (low cognitive levels) of a topic before more in-depth assessment questions are asked on the topic.

Structure of Short Answer Questions

Short Answer Questions do not have a generic structure. Questions may require answers such as complete the sentence, supply the missing word, short descriptive or qualitative answers, diagrams with explanations etc. The answer is usually short, from one word to a few lines. Often students may answer in bullet form.

Example

1. MHz measures the ___________________ of the computer.
2. List the different types of plastic surgery procedures.
3. In economics, state Greshamï¿½s Law.

Advantages of Short Answer Questions

- Short Answer Questions are relatively fast to mark and can be marked by different assessors, as long as the questions are set in such a way that all alternative answers can be considered by the assessors.
- Short Answer Questions are also relatively easy to set compared to many assessment methods.
- Short Answer Questions can be used as part of a formative and summative assessment, as the structure of short answer questions are very similar to examination questions, students are more familiar with the practice and feel less anxious.
- Unlike MCQs, there is no guessing on answers, students must supply an answer.

Disadvantages of Short Answer Questions

- Short Answer Questions (SAQ) are only suitable for questions that can be answered with short responses. It is very important that the assessor is very clear on the type of answers expected when setting the questions, because SAQ is an open-ended questions, students are free to answer any way they choose, short-answer questions can lead to difficulties in grading if the question is not worded carefully.
- Short Answer Questions are typically used for assessing knowledge only, students may often memorize Short Answer Questions with rote learning. If assessors wish to use Short Answer Questions to assess deeper learning, careful attention (and many practices) on appropriate questions are required.
- Accuracy of assessment may be influenced by handwriting/spelling skills
- There can be time management issues when answering Short Answer Questions

How to design a good Short Answer Question?

1. Design short answer items which are appropriate assessment of the learning objective
2. Make sure the content of the short answer question measures knowledge appropriate to the desired learning goal
3. Express the questions with clear wordings and language which are appropriate to the student population
4. Ensure there is only one clearly correct answer in each question
5. Ensure that the item clearly specifies how the question should be answered (e.g. Student should answer it briefly and concisely using a single word or short phrase? Is the question given a specific number of blanks for students to answer?)
6. Consider whether the positioning of the item blank promote efficient scoring
7. Write the instructions clearly so as to specify the desired knowledge and specificity of response
8. Set the questions explicitly and precisely.
9. Direct questions are better than those which require completing the sentences.
10. For numerical answers, let the students know if they will receive marks for showing partial work (process based) or only the results (product based), also indicated the importance of the units.

11. Let the students know what your marking style is like, is bullet point format acceptable, or does it have to be an essay format?
12. Prepare a structured marking sheet; allocate marks or part-marks for acceptable answer(s).
13. Be prepared to accept other equally acceptable answers, some of which you may not have predicted.

Marking Rubrics

Short answer questions tend to be short, and have more precise answers, thus, it is possible for each question to list out all the possible answers/points.

A simple Short Answer Questions Rubric:

Simple Short Answer Questions

5

4

3

2

1

Total

Defining Answers/Points:

Answer all points

75% of all the points answered

50% of all the points answered

25% of all the points answered

0% of all the points answered

For example, if there are 6 possible arguments to a question, and the student scores all 6 arguments, he will get full mark in that question. If he scores only 4 arguments, he will get a relative mark. You may also decide to be lenient, if there are 6 arguments in a question, and the student scores any 4 out of 6, he will get full mark, this would be an assessor decision, however, this decision must be clear and consistent.

If a more essay type of answer is requested, the following rubric maybe suitable: (From Rubric Studio, http://www.rcampus.com/rubricshowc.cfm?b=%25%2D%2B%3B2R%5D8%20%0A&sp=yes&)

MARKING RUBRICS

Excellent

Proficient

Average

Poor

Definition:

Definition is strong and clear.

Some details and definition is generally correct.

Limited or weak definition.

Question has not been attempted or answer is completely incorrect.

Supporting Details:

Many additional details to support definition or concept.

Additional details show understanding of concept.

Some extra information.

Few or no details, only slightly related to topic.

Writing Conventions:

Skillful control of language and mechanics. Sentence structure is strong and effective in communicating information.

Generally acceptable vocabulary, relates to topic. Few spelling/grammatical errors that do not affect meaning.

Some vocabulary related to topic. Some grammatical errors related to spelling, punctuation.

Limited or inappropriate use of vocabulary rleated to topic. Many errors in spelling and grammar.

What is an Oral Assessment?

An oral assessment is a direct means of assessing studentsï¿½ learning outcomes by questioning them. Unlike interviews which usually have a structured question list, oral assessment does not usually have a structured list of questions; assessors ask questions and request responses depending on the circumstances.

There are three typical types of oral assessments:

1. Oral assessment after a direct observation assessment

   An oral assessment is often used as part of a de-briefing session after a practical has been observed. The time duration is usually 3-5 minutes. There is usually no formal structure, assessors usually ask questions as they foresee, however, assessors may plan some general questions in which all students will encounter during the practical.

2. Oral in the form of a viva voce

   A viva voce is the Latin name for oral examination, often given for a university examination with spoken questions and answers. It is usually used to describe the oral examination at a postgraduate level, conducted after the submission of the thesis for a research degree to ensure that the candidate knows enough about the subject to make it at least plausible that the dissertation is his own work. Vivas are traditionally conducted by an external and an internal examiner. There is no set time limit for a viva voce, but a full day examination is often normal.

3. Oral/Aural in a language setting

   Oral in a language setting is a direct speaking test geared at assessing a student's level of speaking proficiency. Aural in a language setting is a listening test (often by devices such as tapes) geared at assessing a student's level of hearing proficiency.

Questions ask in classroom setting do not contribute as oral assessments, as not all students have the benefits of being assessed.

Structure of Oral Assessment

The structure of an oral assessment depends on the type of oral assessment, but in general, the followings are used.

1. Depend on which type of oral assessments, it is sometimes desirable to allow the student to start the oral assessment by giving an account of the analysis of the practice. The sophistication of his spontaneous account can reveal far more than simply his responses to the questions. Questions such as: How do you think you did?

2. Probing questions to initiate and engage the student in conversation. Questions such as: How did you know that? What method did you use to arrive with that conclusion?

3. Prompting questions to give hints that point the student to the right direction to clarify his response, this however does not mean the assessor answers the questions himself. Questions such as: Remember the experiment on What do you think this relates to?

4. Challenging questions to assess the deep understanding - the higher level of Blooms taxonomy. Questions such as: Can you justify why your method is more efficient than Prof. Einstein

Advantages of Oral Assessment

- There can be no plagiarism or false reports.
- Assessors receive immediate reactions and responses.
- It complements perfectly with practical assessments.

Disadvantages of Oral Assessment

- Oral assessment is very time-consuming, it is an expensive way of assessing.
- Validity is high but reliability is not. Clear assessment criteria and grading are required for all parties so that students and assessors are fully aware of how the performance will be judged to increase reliability.
- There are rarely any clear guidelines about what is fair to judge at a viva. There have been some contentious cases that the assessor has rejected (?) or even failed a dissertation because the assessor is unwilling to accept the results of a candidate due to difference in opinions. Although there will be examiners' reports, there is rarely any record of the process itself to ensure its fairness.
- Oral assessment may present significant difficulties for international students or students with certain impairments, who may require access to an alternative type of assessment that provides an acceptable test of learning outcomes. Students with some other impairments may be able to undertake oral assessment but may require some adjustments in order to have an equal footing.
- Immediate feedback is useful, but sometimes that is difficult due to time constraints.
- Oral assessment is usually ephemeral, and dissenting views may later be contested if notes or recordings are not documented clearly.

How to design a good Oral Assessment?

1. Ensure the students know what the objectives of the assessment are.
2. Provide students the time period, location, guidelines, requirements, assessment criteria and if there are items that are not to be included. The students should also be aware of who is going to assess them ï¿½ tutor, peers and/or self? And if peers or themselves are going to assess, would the weightings be the same as the tutor's assessment?
3. Prepare a structured marking sheet for all assessors.
4. Give sufficient time for students to respond.
5. Teacher should incorporate oral assessment into the practice of teaching during class, e.g. how to think out loud.

Marking Rubrics

Below is a sample of marking rubrics and grading standards for an oral assessment after a direct observation assessment:

MARKING RUBRICS
Excellent
Proficient
Average
Poor
Content:
Relates to topic, detailed, and accurate
All content directly related to the topic. Opinions were always supported by fact if possible.
Content directly related to the topic. Almost all opinions were supported by facts.
Demonstrated Basic understanding of the topic. Many opinions were not supported by facts.
Few facts related to the topic. Most Information was opinion.
Knowledge:
Demonstrate knowledge of subject
Showed a thorough knowledge of the topic. Able to use assessor questions to further demonstrate understanding of the topic. Appeared to be an expert on the subject being presented
Showed a working knowledge of the topic. Able to satisfactorily answer assessor questions and provided additional information upon request.
Showed basic knowledge of the topic. Able to address assessor questions by repeating parts of the presentation - did not provide any additional information.

Showed little or no knowledge of the topic. Unable to answer assessor questions or comment further on any part of the presentation.

Posture/Eye Contact:

Appropriate posture and effective eye contact

Stood upright and appeared confident throughout. Avoided rocking, shifting, and other nervous behavior. Made eye contact throughout the assessors.

Posture was good for most of the presentation. Made eye contact numerous times during presentation. Did not rely too heavily on notes or visual aids.

Sometimes rocked, shifted, or appeared uncomfortable. Made occasional eye contact with one or two audience members. Did not rely too heavily on notes or visual aids

Posture was poor. Slouched, shifted from foot to foot, and appeared very uncomfortable. Made almost no eye contact with the audience. Looked down at notes or visual aids.

Enthusiasm:

Energetic, confident, not frenetic

Appeared enthusiastic and confident at all times. Moderated level of excitement to hold audience's attention.

Appeared enthusiastic and confident at all times. May have appeared overly enthusiastic at times. Held audience interest for most of the time.

Showed some confident and little excitement about the topic. Attempted to modify behavior to engage audience on one or more occasions. Lost attention of some audience members.

Showed little or no enthusiasm about the topic. Nervous. Did not moderate level of excitement in response to audience reaction. Lost audience interest.

Audience:

Engage and interact with audience

Moderated speaking style based on audience feedback. Calmly and eloquently addressed audience questions and comments. Engaged audience for the duration of the presentation.

Adjusted volume, pace, and enthusiasm several times. Answered audience questions and addressed comments. Presenter adjusted enthusiasm or pace to hold audience attention.

Spoke more loudly when requested by audience members. Presenter was clearly uncomfortable. Presenter attempted to adjust enthusiasm or pace to hold audience attention.

Did not adjust speaking style based on audience reaction. Could not answer audience questions. Presenter made no visible effort to hold audience interest.

Pace:

Speaks at an appropriate pace

Speaker adjusted pace to stay within allotted time. Speaker answered audience questions without overdo it or covered additional material if there were no questions

Speaker's pace was appropriate throughout

Tended to speak too quickly or too slowly.

Consistently spoke too fast or too slow.

Below is another sample of marking rubrics and grading standards for an oral assessment after a direct observation assessment (From Swarthmore College, Friends Select School, Rubrics, 2008)

MARKING RUBRICS

Excellent

Proficient

Average

Poor

Content:

Speaker consistently uses the appropriate functions and vocabulary necessary to communicate

Speaker generally uses the appropriate functions and vocabulary necessary to communicate.

Speaker sometimes uses the appropriate functions and vocabulary necessary to communicate.

Speaker uses few of the appropriate functions and vocabulary necessary to communicate.

Accuracy:

Speaker uses language correctly, including grammar, spelling, word order, and punctuation.

Speaker usually uses language correctly, including grammar, spelling, word order, and punctuation.

Speaker has some problems with language usage.

Speaker makes many errors in language usage.

Fluency:

Speaker speaks clearly without hesitation. Pronunciation and intonation sound natural.

Speaker has few problems with hesitation, pronunciation, and/or intonation.

Speaker has some problems with hesitation, pronunciation, and/or intonation.

Speaker hesitates frequently and struggles with pronunciation and intonation.

Comprehensibility:

Listener understands all of what the speakers are trying to communicate.

Listener understands most of what the speakers are trying to communicate.

Listener understands less than half of what the speakers are trying to communicate.

Listener understands little of what the speakers are trying to communicate.

What is a Direct Observation?

Direct Observation assessment is exactly as the name suggested ï¿½ the assessors observe the students performing the assessment and see if they have the ability to perform it properly. Practical skills particularly clinical related areas often use direct observation to assess students. Group work such as problem based learning may sometimes use direct observation to judge a student's input. Observation assessment is only effective when it follows a systematic plan to help both the assessor and the student focus on what needed to be observed and recorded. An oral assessment is often used as a follow-up assessment to supplement any questions. Sometimes, there is no effective alternative to direct observation.

Structure of Direct Observation Assessment

The structure of an observation assessment greatly depends on the discipline in which the assessment takes place, it also depends on whether the assessor is observing the entire work or only part of the work. In general, the assessor will observe for 5 -10 minutes, make a field note to help with the feedback and grading. This maybe followed by an interview/oral assessment.

Advantages of Direct Observation

- Observation may sometimes be the only assessment method possible.
- There can be no plagiarism or false reports.
- It is a great way to assess practical skills.

Disadvantages of Direct Observation

- Direct observation does not assess the higher-order levels of learning outcomes, and is often not adequate for a full assessment; oral questioning or other supplementary assessments may be required.
- Direct observation assessment requires a lot of time to assess and to prepare thus, it is an expensive way of assessing.
- The presence of the observer can change student's performance as being watched can be intimidating for many students. Furthermore, the dynamics of the observation room may change as the observer/assessor enters. It is often debatable whether the observer/assessor should be visible or hidden. So where, who and how the observation is being assessed are all factors which may affect a good observation assessment.
- There is no anonymity in Direct Observation.

- To ensure high efficiency and reliability, clear grading standards for all parties are essential. However, grading criteria for observation assessment can be trivial to design and develop.
- Immediate feedback is useful, but sometimes that is difficult due to time constraints.
- Practical work is usually ephemeral and dissenting views may later be contested if notes or recordings are not documented clearly.
- It can sometimes be subjective.

How to design a good Direct Observation Assessment?

1. Ensure students know what the objectives of the observation assessment are.
2. Provide students the time period, location, guidelines, requirements, assessment criteria and if there are items that are not to be included. Students should also be aware of who is going to assess them ï¿½ tutor, peers and/or self? And if peers or themselves are going to assess, would the weightings be the same as the tutor's assessment?
3. Prepare a structured marking sheet for all assessors.
4. Feedback is very important for a good observation assessment.

Marking Rubrics

As direct observation is usually assessed on practical type of work, below is a sample rubric for a direct observation assessment in a laboratory. As mentioned before, the grading criteria changes depending whether the assessor is observing the entire work or only part of the work.

(From Recipe for Success, accessed 05 July 2008

http://myt4l.com/index.php?v=pl&page_ac=view&type=tools&tool=rubricmaker)

MARKING RUBRICS

Excellent

Proficient

Average

Poor

Lab Work-Purpose:

Defines goal of experiment

Used clear, accurate language to restate question or problem in student's own words. Provided examples of similar experiments.

Used proper vocabulary to state question or problem.

Stated question or problem using incorrect vocabulary. Did not state problem in student's own words.

Did not state question or problem.

Lab Work-Hypothesis:

Prediction between experiment and results

Obvious connection between the problem and predicted outcome. Provided references showing that hypothesis refutes or defends established knowledge. Variables were identified and classified as dependent and independent.

Hypothesis and problem were clearly connected. Hypothesis refuted or defended established knowledge. Variables were identified and classified as dependent and independent.

No connection between hypothesis and experiment. No clear way to prove or disprove hypothesis by performing experiment. Variables were not completely described or were incorrectly classified as dependent or independent.

Hypothesis was missing or was unrelated to the experiment. Did not mention dependent and independent variables.

Lab Work-Materials and Equipment:

List of materials used

Made complete list of materials used. Explained why materials were chosen.

Made complete list of materials used. Showed information about size and units of measurement.

Did not list one or two items used. Did not show details about items used.

List of materials was missing or showed only a few of the materials used.

Lab Work-Methods:

Description of process and setup

Setup was documented completely. Method was also documented completely and accurately, making experiment easy to reproduce.

Setup included descriptive text and diagrams were provided if appropriate. Experiment can be reproduced using the steps provided.

Description was general or did not include diagrams. Procedure was missing multiple steps. Information provided is not sufficient to replicate experiment.

Setup was not described or documented. Step-by-step procedure was missing or inadequate.

Lab Work-Data Quality:

Accurate measurement and labeling

All data was complete and accurately labeled. Data sampled at appropriate intervals as defined in Methods section of lab report.

All data was complete and accurately labeled. Data was sampled at appropriate intervals.

Data was incomplete. Some data was not labeled using appropriate units of measure. Data sampling intervals inadequate to support hypothesis.

Included little or no relevant data. Data was not labeled using appropriate units of measure. Data sampling intervals were random or inadequate.

Lab Work-Data Analysis:

Student analyzed data and identified trends

Identified and described trends and made appropriate conclusions based on the data. Used statistical techniques to identify and disregard flawed data. Showed calculations.

Identified valid trends and made appropriate conclusions based on the data. Documented calculations made during data analysis.

Only identified obvious trends or found trends not fully supported by the data.

Trends were missing or were not supported by the data collected. Obvious trends were overlooked.

Lab Work-Safety:

Follows rules and uses good judgment

Followed all safety rules and wrote about safety in lab report.

Followed all safety rules.

Did not follow all safety rules.

Did not follow safety rules and caused a dangerous situation.

Lab Work-Conclusion:

Summarizes findings and compares actual results with expected results

Restated problem and hypothesis. Justified design and methods of experiment. Findings were discussed in detail. Conclusions directly address hypothesis. Statements and conclusions were supported by the data.

Problem was restated. Statements and conclusions were based on the data collected. Showed a strong relationship between conclusions and hypothesis.

Problem was restated. Conclusions were simplistic. No clear relationship between conclusions and hypothesis.

Original problem was not restated. Findings were not summarized. Conclusions were not relevant to hypothesis.

Web Reference and Resources

What is a Presentation?

Presentation is the process of showing and explaining the content of a topic to an audience or a group of audiences. It is often used to assess student learning in individual or group research projects. In recent times, presentation is no longer just about oral presentation but also visuals. Paper, white board or PowerPoint presentation are sample tools to aid the visual part of the presentation. Peer and tutor assessment can be used as part of the grading process, this would allow open-mindedness particularly if the topic or presentation style generates subjective opinions or different views.

Structure of Presentation

Presentation assessment usually consists of a topic for the student to research, discuss and present. Question and answer session is usually included after the presentation. This measures the ability of students to respond, think under pressure and manage discussion. Sometimes it is in this part of the presentation that the student shows his/her in-depth knowledge of the topic and presentation skills. A good presentation is usually expected to consist of

1. Introduction/ Aims/Objectives
2. Major points and ideas explained and summarized
3. Results/Related points/Issues/or others depending on the topic
4. Conclusion - future work
5. The presentation should be present in the time allowed

Advantages of Presentation

- Humans tend to remember actions and behaviors easier than words through reading, writing and listening. Observing others peers presenting will help students reflect on oneself and avoid repeating others' mistakes. And at the same time, students can learn from others' good work.
- Presentation is an effective method to improve students at public speaking.
- Presentation is often part of the overall assessment for a research thesis, it helps to give detailed summary of the research project to the assessors and also allow the assessors to question the student with an immediate response at a more in-depth level which they may not find in the thesis report.

Disadvantages of Presentation

- Presentation does not take a long time to mark but it does take relative amount of time for the students to present during contact hours, thus this is usually not the best method for a large class.
- It is important for the assessors to state the assessment criteria explicitly, the students need to know if the content of the material is part of the criteria and/or the method of presenting is part of the criteria. If students are to be assessed on different aspects other than the content, they should be given the opportunity to learn about and practice those aspects before being assessed.
- If the skills of live presentation are not relevant to the learning outcomes, presentation may not be a suitable assessment method.
- Students may overspend their time on flashy animation, software and other high-tech sound effects, and not on the actual knowledge contents. Tutor and peer assessors may also be affected by these effects and overlook the meaningful ideas behind the topic.

How to design a good Presentation Assessment?

1. Ensure the students know what the primary objective of the presentation assessment is.
2. Tell them how long the presentation will be, and let them know if there is time for Q&A.
3. Let students know the assessment criteria and marking scheme, the students should also be aware of who is going to assess them – tutor, peers and/or self? And if peers or themselves are going to assess, would the weightings be the same as the tutor's assessment?
4. Prepare a structured marking sheet for all assessors.

Marking Rubrics

There are many different grading criteria standards, to design the best grading standards for your presentation assessment, you must keep in mind the learning outcomes of the assessment. Entertaining; relevant and useful; knowledgeable; involved the audience; well organized; well prepared; easy to understand; confident are all factors that determine a good presentation.

A generic presentation grading standard is shown below:

MARKING RUBRICS

Excellent

Proficient

Average

Poor

Content:

Relates to topic, detailed, and accurate

All content directly related to the topic. Opinions were always supported by fact if possible.

Content directly related to the topic. Almost all opinions were supported by facts.

Demonstrated Basic understanding of the topic. Many opinions were not supported by facts.

Few facts related to the topic. Most Information was opinion.

Knowledge:

Demonstrate knowledge of subject

Showed a thorough knowledge of the topic. Able to use assessor questions to further demonstrate understanding of the topic. Appeared to be an expert on the subject being presented

Showed a working knowledge of the topic. Able to satisfactorily answer assessor questions and provided additional information upon request.

Showed basic knowledge of the topic. Able to address assessor questions by repeating parts of the presentation - did not provide any additional information.

Showed little or no knowledge of the topic. Unable to answer assessor questions or comment further on any part of the presentation.

Posture/Eye Contact/Mannerism:

Appropriate posture and effective eye contact

Stood upright and appeared confident throughout. Avoided rocking, shifting, and other nervous behavior. Made eye contact throughout the assessors.

Posture was good for most of the presentation. Made eye contact numerous times during presentation. Did not rely too heavily on notes or visual aids.

Sometimes rocked, shifted, or appeared uncomfortable. Made occasional eye contact with one or two audience members. Did not rely too heavily on notes or visual aids

Posture was poor. Slouched, shifted from foot to foot, and appeared very uncomfortable. Made almost no eye contact with the audience. Looked down at notes or visual aids.

Enthusiasm:

Energetic, confident, not frenetic

Appeared enthusiastic and confident at all times. Moderated level of excitement to hold audience's attention.

Appeared enthusiastic and confident at all times. May have appeared overly enthusiastic at times. Held audience interest for most of the time.

Showed some confidence and little excitement about the topic. Attempted to modify behavior to engage audience on one or more occasions. Lost attention of some audience members.

Showed little or no enthusiasm about the topic. Nervous. Did not moderate level of excitement in response to audience reaction. Lost audience interest.

Audience:

Engage and interact with audience

Moderated speaking style based on audience feedback. Calmly and eloquently addressed audience questions and comments. Engaged audience for the duration of the presentation.

Adjusted volume, pace, and enthusiasm several times. Answered audience questions and addressed comments. Presenter adjusted enthusiasm or pace to hold audience attention.

Spoke more loudly when requested by audience members. Presenter was clearly uncomfortable. Presenter attempted to adjust enthusiasm or pace to hold audience attention.

Did not adjust speaking style based on audience reaction. Could not answer audience questions. Presenter made no visible effort to hold audience interest.

Pace:

Speaks at an appropriate pace

Speaker adjusted pace to stay within allotted time. Speaker answered audience questions without overdo it or covered additional material if there were no questions.

Speaker's pace was appropriate throughout

Tended to speak too quickly or too slowly

Consistently spoke too fast or too slow

Timing:

Length of Presentation Length of Q&A

Perfect timing

Adequate Timing

Too short or too long

Finish abruptly

What are Practical Experiments?

The aim of arranging practical experiments for students is to develop students' general and specific skills to carry out scientific experiments, and to enhance their practical competence in handling experimental instrumentations. Practical experiment constitutes an important part in the research cycle for scientific inquiries, which provides the empirical basis for the establishment and refinement of theories and indications for making predictions. It makes sure that students do not only learn the body of scientific knowledge, but also the methods in which it has been developed from.

Structure of Practical Experiments

The objective of an experiment usually involves testing the validity of hypotheses generated base on theories. In the usual settings, students are normally given the experimental design and procedures, and are asked to carry out the experiment by following the given instructions carefully. When carrying out experiments, teachers and demonstrators would offer help and support to the students with the equipments and give advices regarding their experimental techniques. The students have to deduce the hypotheses being tested from the given experimental design, to collect the data and take measurements accurately in the experimental tasks, to analyze and interpret the results, and also to summarize and evaluate the experiment in a written report.

Some teachers may arrange student-designed experiments in their courses. In this setting, students have to formulate testable hypotheses based on the topics covered in the course. They also have to design, present and explain their experimental methodology to the teachers. The description of the method needs to be unambiguous and concise, and provides sufficient details for someone else to replicate the experiment by merely reading the instructions. The teacher can assess students' experimental design skills at this stage, as well as giving feedback and suggesting precautions and modifications for students. The students will then conduct the experiment based on the modified design.

Advantages of Practical Experiments

- Allows students to demonstrate and practice their knowledge and skills of 'how to do something' in action, and to achieve the learning outcomes by themselves, which is not feasible through written assessments such as free-

response questions or multiple-choice questions
- Provides a powerful tool for teachers to objectively assess the competence of these manual skills of the students
- Establishes the link between theories and practice; students can learn the scientific attitude of taking and analyzing data patiently and accurately; experiments do not replace textbooks and lectures, but enhance learning with practical experience
- Practical experiments can be extended to become a hands-on experimental skills examination, to be coupled with brief instructions and interactive questions on theories

Disadvantages of Practical Experiments

- It is time-consuming and costly to set up laboratory experiments and the necessary instrumentations along with adequate technical support; close supervision and help may be needed for students who lack confidence in doing practical experiments
- For some experiments, it may not be feasible for the faculty to offer one set of equipments to each student; students will have to perform the experiment as a group, which may give rise to unfair distribution of work in the group
- Teachers may find it difficult to develop uniform, fair, and reliable assessment rubrics to evaluate students‘ practical skills

How to design a good Practical Experiment Assessment?

1. Before conducting the practical experiment sessions, teachers can offer a briefing session to explain to the class the basic theoretical background, learning outcomes, and the required techniques of the experiment. Precautions, potential problems and hazards, and safety issues must be carefully discussed and explained to students in the briefing session.
2. The experimental sessions can be coupled with active and interactive assessments in relation to the theories. In this setting, instructions can be given to students to carry out the experiment. Upon the observation of results, students need to answer questions to explain the immediate observations based on the principles and theories they have learnt.
3. Teachers should be reminded not to arrange practical experiments that require excessively costly, unrealistic or unfeasible equipments.
4. In the examination context, teachers may consider video-taping the students' performance in the experiment for easier assessment and to allow multiple assessors to rate the students' performance.

Marking Rubrics
MARKING RUBRICS
Excellent
Proficient
Average
Poor
Relevance and feasibility of experimental design:
Hypothesis was stated concisely and specifically; the experimental design can efficiently test the validity of the stated hypothesis
Hypothesis was stated clearly, but was not very specific; the experimental design is valid for testing the hypothesis
Hypothesis stated was ambiguous and not specific enough; the experimental design is weakly linked to the testing of the hypothesis
No hypothesis is stated for testing; the objective of performing the experiment is unknown
Experimental techniques:

Experimental tasks were done in an organized and effective way; apparatus were handled competently with confidence; all given instructions were followed tightly

Most of the experimental tasks were done neatly and satisfactorily; possess knowledge of how to handle most of the necessary apparatus and procedures appropriately; instructions were well-followed

Only some of the experimental tasks were done satisfactorily; have frequent problems in handling some of the apparatus and procedures, and also in following the given instructions

Experiment was done chaotically, without knowledge of how to use and handle the apparatus appropriately; do not follow the experimental instructions

Scientific attitude and safety issues:

Taking the experiment with a serious attitude; data and measurements were made accurately and patiently; having thought carefully about possible improvements of the design while performing the tasks

Taking the experiment with a positive attitude; observations and measurements were made with minor errors; tried to think about limitations of the experimental design

Doing the experiment for fun; results were taken with large errors; did not try to think about the rationale behind the experiment

Fooling around with the experimental equipments; results were estimated without basing on real data

What is Case Study?

Case study is a learning practice that shifts the emphasis from lecture-based activities towards more student-based activities. In general, teaching materials for case study can come from various sources. Teaching materials can be a short journal or news article; they can be a scenario of problem solving and decision making; they can be an open-ended question, a picture or even a diagram. The aim of case study is to help students demonstrate the theoretical concepts in real-life issues. Students can also develop various generic skills, such as decision making and practical skills through the case study. Case study can be practiced either individually or as a group. Students are actively involved in the learning process because they are required to produce solution and arguments for their study. Case study can reinforce the traditional teaching and learning methods because it acts as a bridge between theory and practice.

Structure of Case Study

A case study may consist of the following sections:

- **Objective:** The expected learning outcomes of the case that teachers want their students to develop (e.g. the application to the theory into a scenario).
- **Description of the case:** The way a teacher presents the case. It can be in the forms of diagram, newspaper journals and a scenario presented within a short paragraph. Of course, the case may not always be an exact mimic of real-life scenario. It is also possible that the case study is presented with some questions and instructions. Thus, the students can understand what is happening in the case and what they are trying to achieve.
- **Preparation and Analysis:** Some teachers may prefer providing the case study and some related questions to students prior class. Students have to prepare research materials and analyze the piece given in their own time, this will help reduce preparatory work during class time and also provide opportunities for the teacher to give valuable feedback.
- **Discussion:** If case study is practiced as a group activity, students can discuss their analysis and opinions with other group members. Students can be divided into different groups. For example, if the case is about the legislation of statutory minimum wage, then group A can look at the issue from the Governmentï¿½s perspective, group B can look at the issue from employersï¿½ perspective, and Group C can look at the issue from the employeesï¿½ perspective.
- **Presentation:** It refers to the ways students present their opinions and findings. Students may be asked to report their analysis, findings and discussion through short presentation, poster, essay, debate and worksheet.
- **Conclusion:** Students conclude their findings and their views of the case.
- **Feedback:** Once everything is done, teachers can give some feedback on studentsï¿½ performance.

Advantages of Case Study

- An opportunity to apply the theoretical concepts to a real-life scenario
- Encourage active and group learning
- Develop generic skills such as decision making, problem solving and collaboration skills
- The mimic of real-life scenario may enhance students' engagement to the subject
- Stimulate students to carry out independent research outside the classroom
- Practice time management because students need to discuss and decide how to best carry out the work in class

Disadvantages of Case Study

- Some teachers may be reluctant to change to this new teaching modules (prefer talk and chalk approach)
- Time consuming to look for or create a case
- Students may be unfamiliar with this teaching and learning approach, teachers may need to take some time to explain the instructions
- Quieter students may find this approach challenging because they may have to work with other students

How to design a good Case Study Assessment?

1. Decide the topics, objectives, skills and learning outcomes that students will accomplish
2. Create a case that students can apply the theoretical concept, ensure it is actually feasible
3. Make sure the case fit into the context of the subject
4. Decide the case study to be practiced as individual activity or group activity
5. Assign the case to students before class, so that they have to do their research outside the class, or give the case to students in class, so that they can brainstorm ideas in class, or even ask students to look for a case based on their interests
6. Teachers only supervise the in-class activity but do not give too much support or help
7. Provide a few questions for students to do their analysis. This assists and guides students to develop "the best strategy" for problem solving in the case
8. Be aware of the time allocation (such as the time for preparation and discussion)
9. Provide feedback and comments on students' performance after the activity has been finished
10. Prepare for unexpected outcomes to emerge. As real-life cases are complex and open to different disciplines and opinions, there may be no right or authoritative answer in some scenarios, students may give answers that are innovative and out of the course context
11. Invite people from related industries to supervise the activity. For example, if the case is about the safety crisis of a nuclear plant, teachers can invite some people from nuclear engineering to supervise the activity and share their first- hand experiences in relation to the case
12. Make sure to provide guidelines and explanations to students as some of them may be unfamiliar with this teaching and learning approach
13. Clear grading criteria
14. Decide the way students would present their analysis. After students have finished their analysis, they have to share their findings and opinions with other teacher and students. They can present their work in the forms of oral presentation, short summary, poster and even debate with other groups. Teachers have to decide the form of presentation because they assess their students based on those presentation and poster

Marking Rubrics

As there are many different approaches to practice Case Study, there are different assessment criteria. Teachers have to make sure the learning outcomes are aligned with the case for analysis (e.g. a scenario analysis or diagram analysis). In addition, teachers have to ensure that the grading criteria fit the format chosen for the case. Here is a sample marking rubrics for case study.

MARKING RUBRICS

Excellent

Proficient

Average

Poor

Understand and apply the theory:

Showed a thorough understanding of the theory; able to concisely assess the case to apply the theoretical concept at a deep level

Showed a working understanding of the theory; able to satisfactorily assess the case but applied the theoretical concept at a surface level

Showed basic understanding of the theory; attempted to assess the case and apply the theoretical concept in a very limited level

Showed little understanding of the theory; poorly assessed the case and applied the theoretical concept

Problem solving skills:

Able to suggest and bring out appropriate solutions to the case; many solutions were provided; logical approach to seek for solutions was observed

Able to bring out some solutions; logical flow was still observed but there was a lack of relevance of the flow

Still able to bring out a few solutions on time; logical flow was hardly observed

Failed to bring out any solution to the case; logical flow was not observed

Creative opinions and solutions:

Able to come up with some innovative opinions; solutions were not those mentioned on textbook and lesson

Attempted to look for a few innovative opinions, some solutions were those not mentioned on textbook and lesson

Attempted to look for any innovative opinions; solutions were those mentioned on textbook and lesson

Failed to show or didnï¿½t attempt to give any innovative opinions; ideas were those on textbook

Case analysis:

A deep and critical analysis was made based on a wild range of inter-disciplinary perspectives

A satisfactory analysis was made; showed the attempt to analyze the case from a wild perspective but not deep and critical enough

Analysis was made based on the subject discipline at a surface level

Failed to make an analysis of the case with the context of the subject

A Case Study Example

- **Length:** 1 hour (one tutorial)
- **Course:** Economics course
- **Aim:** To demonstrate some Economic concepts in the legislation of statutory minimum wage
- **Assessment:** Group work, presentation skills, application of Economic theories
- **Case description:**

An editorial from MingPao (10-11-2009)

Title: Minimum wage should be low

A minimum wage bill is now before the Legislative Council (Legco). The Liberal Party, which represents the business sector, has suggested that the minimum wage should be set at $24 an hour (about $5,000 a month), while most trade unions have demanded that it be at least $33 an hour (about $7,000 a month). This newspaper reported last Wednesday the government intends it to be near the former initially.

The government's idea is in keeping with the reality in Hong Kong. The higher the minimum wage is, the likelier it will be for the employment market to be distorted and for wage earners to lose their jobs. Therefore, the minimum wage should be low initially. It is necessary to observe how seriously the legislation will impact on the employment market before gradually adjusting it in the light of the actual situation.

As that is a mainstream view and a minimum wage bill has been presented to Legco, it is not realistic for business people (employers) to object to legislating for a minimum wage in principle or refuse to discuss how much the minimum wage should be or how the legislation should be enforced in practice. Employers and unionists should try to make a good job of the legislation and make sure that it will protect poorly-paid workers without considerably increasing unemployment.

If the minimum wage is too high, employers may make little profit, and many employees may become jobless. Even unionists cannot deny society may face such a danger. However, if the minimum wage is excessively low, society will only be exposed to the risk of having an ineffective policy. Poverty may still be a problem, but it would not worsen. And the government could then revise the policy to make it more forceful. Having weighed the pros and cons, we believe the minimum wage should be low initially. That would expose society to lower risk.

Minimum wage legislation is new to Hong Kong. It is unclear how it may impact on the employment market. It is therefore realistic to move forward very cautiously and set the minimum wage low initially lest the market should be seriously distorted.

Instruction:

Students will be divided into three different groups (representing the Government, employers and employees). Each group will be given ten minutes to present their ideas. Then, students will have 30 minutes to discuss the issue of the statutory minimum wage.

IX

Information Education and Communication for Health (IEC)

DEFINITION

The act or process of imparting or acquiring general knowledge, developing the powers of reasoning and judgment, and generally preparing oneself or others intellectually for mature life.The knowledge or skill obtained or developed by a learning process.

Health education defined

- "Health education is a process that informs, motivates and helps people to adopt and maintain healthy practices and lifestyles, advocates environmental changes as needed to ssfacilitate this goal and conducts, professional training and research to the same end".
- Health education is any combination of learning experiences designed to help individuals and communities improve their health, by increasing their knowledge or influencing their attitudes

Principles of health education

- Interest
- Participation
- Known to unknown
- Comprehension
- Reinforcement
- Motivation
- Learning by doing
- Good human relations

Introduction

Definition

Definition of Health Education Health education deals with individuals and groups of people to make them learn how to behave in a manner conducive to the promotion, maintenance, or restoration of health. Health education is the process of educating people about health.

The Joint Committee on Health Education and Promotion Terminology (2001) defined Health Education as "any combination of planned learning experiences based on sound theories that provide individuals, groups, and communities the opportunity to acquire information and the skills needed to make quality health decisions." The

World Health Organization defined Health Education as "comprising of consciously constructed opportunities for learning, involving some form of communication designed to improve health literacy, including improving knowledge, and developing life skills which are conducive to individual and community health".

Aims and Objectives of Health Education

Education for health aims to motivate people to improve their living conditions. It aims to develop a sense of responsibility for health as an individual, as a member of a family and as a member of a community. Educating individuals and groups of people about health related matters enables them to behave in a manner conducive to:

- Promotion of health,
- Maintenance of health, and
- Restoration of health, whenever it is spoiled. The main aims and objectives of health education are to help people to:
- Prevent diseases; by informing and educating them the principles of healthy living and modifying their health behaviour(s).
- Maintain health; by providing knowledge and skills and, motivating them to practice desirable health practices.
- Promote health; through adoption of healthy lifestyle.
- Utilize health services; encourage them to use medical and health services provided for their benefit.

Importance of Health Education

The importance of our health is the importance of life itself. Without health, life is no more than a pitiful existence. So, we should study it more and learn how to be healthy and how to avoid illness.

- Health Education increases people's awareness to health issues.
- It favorably influences the people's attitudes to the improvement of health.
- Health education is important because it is needed for changing people's health related behaviour (change towards health and away from disease inducing things).
- Health Education plays a crucial role in the development of a healthy, inclusive and equitable society.
- It relates to all settings, parts and levels of the society (including schools, colleges, universities, the health services, the community and the workplace.

- Now we say that "Your Health is in your Hands!". The government's health departments can not deliver health at the people's door steps. Health is some thing that people have to achieve themselves. The health care persons can only 'enable' them to achieve it.
- Disease pattern in the society is changing. Communicable diseases are being slowly replaced by non-communicable diseases. Many of these do not have a cure.They need long term management i.e. people should learn how to manage their diseases over years and years (e.g. diabetes, hypertension, coronary artery disease, etc.). That means, the patients need health education.
- Democracy is becoming not only a political system, but also a social process. Participatory decision making is being increasingly resorted to. If the decisions are to be taken by people who take health related decisions, all the decision makers have to learn about health! People who work in local, state and national governments, people who run hospital committees, etc. have to gain health related knowledge!
- De-professionalization of healthcare is being emphasized now. People may go to professionals for expert advice and service; but the basic responsibility for health lies with individuals, families and communities. If they do not want to be healthy, they may even spend money to spoil their health (e.g. spending on tobacco, alcohol, addictive drugs, high speed vehicles, etc.). How can health care persons deliver them health on a platter? They have to learn how to be healthy. That is, they need health education..
- These are the days of health promotion and we need to have health promoting public policies. That means all policy makers in the country working in different areas of public life (at different levels of the society) need to

learn about health!

- The national governments and the United Nations Agencies are setting very lofty goals related to health sector (eradication of a disease, control of an ailment, universal coverage of a service, etc.). Often the coverage of health services needs to be achieved in a time-bound manner. Their achievement needs very high levels of health knowledge and awareness in the society. Naturally health education becomes important!

Comparison of Health Education and Counseling

Health education is somewhat like the counseling that we do in clinics. But they are somewhat different. Let us consider how they are similar and how they are different.

Their Similarities: -

- Both aim at changing people's behaviours, in order to reduce risk to health.
- Both use two-way interactions between the provider and the receiver of health information.
- Both rely on communication skills.

Their Differences: -

- Health Education is usually initiated by the educator. Counseling is usually initiated on the request of a distressed client.
- Health Education aims to disseminate information by discussion. Counseling aims to reduce stress by dialogue.
- Health Education is usually for a group or for a mass audience. Counseling is usually on one-to-one basis or involves a small group.
- Health Education is primarily a 'learning process'. Counseling is primarily a 'coping process' meeting the demands of the disease.

Principles of Health Education Some of the principles of health education are listed below: ·
Strive to make 'Real-needs' the 'Felt-needs'.

Guide people from the known to the un-known. Start by telling about something they know already. And relate the new thing that you intend to tell, to things they already know.

Reinforcement (repetition at intervals) leads to comprehension. Telling once is not enough. It is not easy for people to change their behaviour. We should not expect that we tell them once and they will change once for all! We have to keep repeating the same thing. If possible, make others tell the same thing at some other time or place. This reinforces our health message; and helps them in comprehension.

Tell in a planned sequence (for cumulative learning). If we have to tell them something complicated, let us tell it little by little in a sequential manner (means we don't tell everything at one sitting).

Understand that people change their behaviour only after serious consideration. People do not get ready to change their behaviour unless they think that not changing will really lead them into problems.

Frightening people a little may be useful. We may have to at times frighten them about the disease producing condition! But frightening too much is also not good. We have to be truthful and realistic.

- Use multiple methods to promote learning.
- Utilize both individual approach and group approach for convincing people.
- Use locally available resources.

Set up intermediate targets (changing the knowledge, beliefs, attitudes and practices). For example, you want that your diabetic patient should take insulin injections by himself. First you give him knowledge that insulin is more effective than oral drugs. Then tell him that as the oral drugs are not giving full control of the blood glucose, he is more likely to get complications of diabetes in kidneys, eyes, peripheral nerves etc. (this may change his attitude towards insulin). Later, introduce him to some diabetic who is injecting insulin himself (demonstration). Then he may believe that after all, self-injection of insulin may not be so dif cult (belief). Then, one day, under your and the old patient's supervision, let him try injecting himself (trial). If he succeeds, he may adopt the new practice on regular basis (adoption of the new method).

- Ensure comprehension – e.g. language.
- Motivate the people – Don't just impart knowledge; appeal to their emotions! Fear appeal is one method.
- Ensure participation of the person/ community.
- Utilise the services of change agents in the society – e.g. leader, teachers.
- Make sure that you have exemplary behaviour.
- Make educational diagnosis – to know situational speci cation.
- Make strategies for sub-population – e.g. by age, sex.
- Aim at health promotion – not just at health education. Help people in decision making process. 'Signi cant people' of the person have a lot of in uence in his decision making for health.
- **Enhance the self-esteem of your** clients - Try to increase your clients' self respect. Those who have high level of self respect are likely to follow your advice better.
- **Utilize peer-teaching** - People like to learn from their peers (people who are like themselves). A diabetic is more likely to accept injection treatment, if other diabetics advise him. Self help groups like Diabetics associations, Alcoholics anonymous work by utilizing peer teaching.
- **Understand that a new idea spreads in a community** slowly - When we introduce a new idea into a community (e.g. use condom to protect from HIV), it does not spread so fast in the society. It takes some time. First it is adopted by people who are adventurous and creative. They are the ones who adopt the new idea rst. When mass media advertisements come, the idea becomes a social fashion. People who are conservative in nature, who are afraid of adopting something new (unknown thing) and people who are bound to customs and traditions would not like to adopt the new idea.

Important Areas for Health Education
These include:

- Environmental health,
- Physical health,
- Mental health,
- Social health,
- Emotional health,
- Intellectual health, and
- Spiritual health.

Behaviors that Promote Health Here are mentioned some behaviours that promote people's health:

- Adoption of health promoting behaviours: e.g. breast feeding, weaning, oral rehydration, latrines, child spacing, hygiene practices, tooth brushing, taking malaria prophylaxis, etc.
- Reduction of health damaging behaviours: e.g. smoking, bottle feeding, alcohol consumption, accident prone kind of risk taking driving.
- Utilization of health services: e.g. ante-natal services, child health services, immunization, family planning, participating in screening programmes.
- Recognition of early symptoms and prompt self-referral for treatment: e.g. cancer, tuberculosis.
- Following of drug regimes: e.g. six months DOTS treatment for tuberculosis.
- Action for rehabilitation for minimizing further disability.

- Action to improve sanitation and hygiene: e.g. washing hands with soap, not eating unhygienic food on road side.
- Stages of Behavioural Change Changing people's behavior is a slow process. It involves the following stages:

- Stage of Awareness: The person gets very general information about the new issue. As a result of this, he/she may develop interest in the issue.
- Stage of Interest: The person seeks more information.
- Stage of Evaluation: In the light of new information obtained, the person considers pros and cons; and evaluates its usefulness to him. This evaluation results in a decision.
- Stage of Trial: The person may like to try the method. At this stage, as facilitators, we have to support the individual in implementing the decision effectively and ensure success.
- Stage of Adoption: If the individual is satis ed with the outcome of the trial, he/ she may adopt the material/process permanently.

Methods of Health Education

Individual and family health education

- Group health education

  - Lectures :-
  - Group discussions:-
  - Panel discussions:-
  - Workshop:-
  - Demonstrations:-

- Education of the general pubic

  - Television
  - Radio
  - Press
  - Health Magazines
  - Posters
  - Health exhibition

Approaches to Health Education

A. Individual approach Health education is provided either in the hospital, school, and workplace or at the home of the patient.

- Providing health education has traditionally been the prerogative of the treating physicians and nurses. But now we feel that health education is the job of all the health care personnel.
- General Healthcare Assistants (GHAs) have more contact and thus more opportunity to disseminate the health related information. So, a GHA has to prepare himself/ herself for playing the role of Health Educator.
- The health educator must first create an atmosphere of friendship and allow the individual to talk as much as possible.
- Being good listener is important.
- The advantage of the individual approach lies in the fact that the educator can discuss, argue and persuade the individual to change his/her health related behaviour for the better.

(B) Group Approach The educator talks to a group of people. This can be of many types:

- **Lecture**: This is the traditional method of teaching as happens in the classroom. It is usually de ned as an oral presentation of relevant information by a quali ed person to an audience. Lectures can be made more effective by exhibits. –
- **Group Discussion:** A very effective method, where a group of people (usually peers) freely express their views, share information and in uence each other. They ultimately reach a consensus, or a course of action to be followed. Groups usually consist of 5 - 15 members for maximum effectiveness. A group leader or 'moderator' indicates and steps in the discussion during crucial or decisive moments.
- Demonstration of skills: Here, procedures or skills are demonstrated by quali ed persons. This is usually done step by step and with explanation for each step. The aim is to teach the audience how to perform the same procedures or skills. Other methods for group communication include symposiums, workshops, panel discussions and role-playing.

(C). Mass Approach Radio, television, internet and print media reach and communicate the masses, and cover large population in short time. Mass media is most cost effective. It is primarily used to generate awareness and disseminate facts among masses. It needs to be supplemented with individual and group approach to facilitate adoption of healthy practices. It must also be supported by quality health services to achieve the desirable success.

Types of Appeals in Health Education

The Appeal: The way the content of the message is organized to persuade/convince people.

- Logical/Factual Appeal: - Conveying need for action by giving facts and gures.
- Fear Appeal: - Frightening people by emphasizing serious outcomes of not taking an action.
- Emotional Appeal: - Arousing emotions, images and feelings.
- Humour Appeal: - Conveying message in a funny way (e.g. cartoon).
- Positive Appeal: - Asking to do something (e.g. breast feeding).
- Negative Appeal: - Asking not to do something (e.g. Don't spit around).

Factors that Influence Our Health

We can not achieve health just by distributing medicines or by doing surgical operations. We have to understand that health is the result of achieving an equilibrium between a number of factors. Our genes, our environment, our behaviour and the health care services we avail, all have in uence on the status of our health. We have to remember this while educating people.

Process of Behaviour Change Educating people so as to infuence and change their health related behaviour is a time consuming process. We should not expect that people will change soon after a health education session. We have to remember that the behaviour change is a slow process. It involves the following steps. Unaware Aware (Informed) Concerned Knowledgeable and skilled Motivated to change Ready to change Trial of new behaviour Maintenance/ adoption of new behaviour Fig: Process of behaviour change.

The example of quitting smoking illustrates the different stages of the model shown. Initially the individual may be unaware about the risks involved in a particular behaviour (smoking, in this example). The rst step in a behaviour change program is to make him aware (about ill effects of smoking). Information should be given in such a way that the person feels it is relevant to him. Then he becomes concerned. Once concerned, he/she may acquire more knowledge and skills by talking to friends, healthcare providers, etc. He now is serious about giving up smoking. This is when he is motivated and is ready to change (i.e. to quit smoking). Readiness to change involves preparing to cope with the negative effects of new behavior (e.g. ridicule from peers). Now he tries the new behaviour, with some anxiety about its success. Based on the response to this new behaviour, he nally decides to adopt the new behaviour (i.e. to quit smoking).

Steps in Planning of Health Education Programme

- Find out the needs and background of the target group; their age, sex, knowledge, skills and education, socioeconomic condition, language they speak, beliefs, values, attitude, their media habits, health problems, felt needs, their common health practices, etc.
- Know the locally available resources; meet in uential people, community leaders.
- Identify the topic; prepare the contents.
- Decide where the health education programme should take place; it could be at a primary health centre, in the hospital ward, at home, in a community centre etc.
- Decide what method to use; one-to-one, small group or large meeting, demonstration, exhibition, drama etc.
- Decide what audio-visual aids would be needed to support the programme; lea ets, models, slides, lm, real objects etc.
- Involve the community in the planning process.
- Decide how you will evaluate the outcome of the health education (short and long term evaluation).

Health Education,

Public Relations and Public Health A health educator is "a professionally prepared individual who serves in a variety of roles and is specifically trained to use appropriate educational strategies and methods to facilitate the development of policies, procedures, interventions, and systems conducive to the health of individuals, groups, and communities" (Joint Committee on Terminology, 2001). As a Health Educator you are here to help and enhance the health of others.

Scope of health education

Health is everybody's concern, our health closely affects our other activities like economy, prosperity, our relationship with others and so on. Thus, health education includes:

- The balanced and nutritive diet and how one should prepare it.
- The need for fresh air, water, ventilation, light, physical exercise, recreation, rest and sleep, etc.
- The habit of cleanliness with regard to body, bodily organs, dress and dweling place.
- Knowledge of the structure and functioning of various organs and systems of the body.
- Information about common diseases, their causes, symptoms, precautionary measure and cure.
- Sanitation of home, school, neighbourhood, community, slums, overcrowded cities, factory areas, markets, villages, etc.
- The sewage system, arrangements for fresh water supply, the sanitary arrangement in the city, health centres and their functioning.

The above points reflects its wide scope and also its inter-linkages with our personal, school and community life.

-

Health Promotion

Health education is a means for promoting health in the community. Health promotion is the process of enabling people to increase control over, and to improve their health. Seven key principles promote health among people, which are:

- Equity: The attainment of health depends substantially on remedying inequalities within and between nations.
- Empowerment: An empowered and actively participating community is essential for the attainment of health.
- Healthy Public Policy: Building healthy public policy and creating supportive environments are needed to facilitate healthy choices.
- Reorientation of Health Services: Medical services must be made more accessible and relevant to population needs; the notion of health service must be rede ned and expanded.

- Inter-sectoral Collaboration: Collaboration between institutions and organisations is necessary to achieve health promotion goals.
- Development of Skills that Empower: Individuals need to acquire a range of health, life and social skills. Such skills facilitate community action. Also they enable individuals to decide empowered choice.

7. Internationalism: Health promotion requires an international perspective. If countries are isolated, they nd it dif cult to achieve Millennium Development Goals (MDGs). Basic Strategies for Health Promotion Three basic strategies for health promotion are to:

- Advocate: To create an environment in which a positive health choice can be made.
- Enable: To encourage positive lifestyle changes by explaining the benefits of change.
- Mediate: To try to mediate between two parties with opposing interests to come to a compromise for the promotion of health.

Relation between Communication, Health Education and HealthPromotion
Let us now understand the relation between communication, health education and health promotion. The flow chart depicted below summaries the relation between them. We need to communicate with people if we have to educate them about health (health education).

- Health promotion is achieved through communication and health education; by doing the ve things listed in the gure below.
- We can help people develop personal skills (e.g. teaching sex workers say 'no' to customers that do not use condoms).
- We can strive to see that health services are reoriented (e.g. make them give more preventive and promotive care).
- We can ask the governments to build healthy public policy (e.g. build sanitary latrines in all market places).
- We can strive to create supportive environment (e.g. by making it easy not to smoke and make smoking dif cult).

We can strengthen community action (e.g. by forming hospital advisory committees). Communication skills are very important if we have to achieve the objective of educating people about health. Health Education is an instrument for promoting health. Health promotion is the ultimate goal of health education.

Communication skills are very important if we have to achieve the objective of educating people about health. Health Education is an instrument for promoting health. Health promotion is the ultimate goal of health education.

Health Education Public Relations and Public Health
Conducting Health Education and Health Promotion in Different Settings The Four Settings for Health Education and Health Promotion Health can be promoted at four different settings: school, hospital, community and work place.

These four settings provide the opportunities to reach key groups. These are depicted in the pictures below. Fig: Four common settings for health promotion: School, Workplace, Hospital and Community. We should learn how to provide health education to people in all these four settings.

Health Promoting School

- **The School:** School health services include screening for health problems, rst aid, referral for health services and counseling.
- **The workplace:** Health can be promoted in the workplace through workplace related health policies, health education for the workers and employers, and implementation of safety standards.
- **The Hospital:** Health can be promoted in hospitals by education of patients, health promotion policies (examples: healthy food, balance between prevention and cure, referral links with primary health care institutions, provision of support for health care workers).
- **The Community:** Improvement in health can be achieved through community involvement and participation.

The term community is used to describe a group of people sharing some interest or a social network of relationship at a local level. It means more than just people who live close together; it implies sharing and working together in some way. Various need based activities may be planned and implemented in community settings to promote their health. Fig: Screening the School Children, for detection of diseases and disabilities. This is an important Health Promotion Activity. Fig: Conducting a hygiene education procession.

Concept of Health Promoting Hospitals (HPHs) A health promoting hospital recognizes the importance of preventing illness and promoting health. It incorporates the principles of health promotion into its work. A health promoting hospital 'integrates health promotion into the role of staff and reorients its role in the community to improve the health of the population. It also has an organisational commitment to the health and wellbeing of patients and their families, and staff. The staff of a HPH work collaboratively with others with the aim of improving the health of patients and their families, and the wider community.'

According to WHO, the principles of a health promoting hospital are:

- The hospital facilitates the health of patients, staff and the community.
- It promotes human dignity and equity.
- Is oriented towards quality improvement.
- It focuses on health in its broader sense, not only disease and curative treatment.
- Contributes to empowerment of patients/clients.
- Forms partnerships with others in health care and the community.
- Uses of resources efficiently and effectively.
- The term health promoting hospitals may seem contradictory and some hospital staff may argue that health promotion is not their job.
- But the concept of a health promoting hospital goes much further than traditional health promotion. In addition, hospitals:

- As providers of expert information to patients/clients and the community, can encourage prevention, self management and foster empowerment.
- As institutions with a large number of workers and service users, can reach a large section of the population (personnel, patients and relatives).
- As centers of modern medicine, research and education that accumulate much knowledge and experience, they can in uence health promotion practices and programs.
- As producers of large amounts of waste, they can contribute to the reduction of environmental pollution and,
- As large-scale consumers, they can favour healthy products and environmental safety.
- Health promoting hospitals also support staff to incorporate the principles of health promotion into their every day work, making health promotion everybody's business.

Health promotion is considered a core quality dimension of hospital services as well as patient safety and clinical effectiveness. Against the rising incidence of chronic diseases, the provision of health promotion services is an important factor for sustained health, quality of life and ef ciency.

The health care staff have to link the hospital to its community. This can be done by changing the culture of hospital care towards interdisciplinary working, transparent decision-making and with active involvement of patients and partners.

Core Competencies for doing Health Promotion Work To do health promotion work, we need to have some competencies.

Roles of a Faculty Nurse Educator in health education

Balancing all the duties required of an educator can be tricky, especially as a member of university faculty.

Not only teachers, nurse educators serve as administrators, advisors, clinical coaches, lab instructors, mentors to new faculty members, course developers, researchers, and more.

It's also crucial that a faculty works together as a team, sharing the load and providing students with a truly exceptional nurse education.

The National Council of State Boards of Nursing (NCSBN) categorizes a nurse educator's duties into three main roles: collaborator, director of student learning, and role model.

Collaborators

Nurse educators are collaborators, capable of bringing others together and building partnerships. Aside from nursing staff, they coordinate student learning with professors across all disciplines.

Nurse educators also prepare students to work as a team in an environment where collaborative relationships have been directly linked to better patient outcomes.

Director of Student Learning

The director of student learning encourages development of staff, program, and curriculum. A faculty member in this role should have graduate level courses in education as well as nursing.

Role Models for Students

Nurse educators provide ongoing mentorship and serve as examples to students through various stages of hands-on learning. It's an especially important role in clinical development, where students look to their teachers for feedback on patient interaction, decision-making, and health assessment.

Role Models for Faculty

Seasoned nurse educators serve as role models for newer faculty as well. By spearheading a culture of learning, nurse educators can inspire each other to improve the delivery of nurse education.

Nurse Educators in a Hospital Setting

A nurse educator's role looks a bit different in a hospital setting. Rather than instructing students who are at the beginning their nurse education, these educators support working, registered nurses through experiential learning.

Fostering Growth

Nurse educators work with their teams and other staff to assess each students' capabilities. This gathering of information, combined with direct observations, allows them to provide feedback on ways the student can improve within the healthcare setting.

Some areas of student evaluation may include:

- Effectiveness in applying person-centered care
- Independently implementing and following up on nursing interventions
- Being able to accurately document patient history, status, diagnosis, actions, and summary of care

In addition to student development, nurse educators also support the professional growth of healthcare teams. This often involves arranging team-building exercises and educational seminars for nursing staff and colleagues.

Role of Nurse's in health education in hospital setting

1. Start right away. Teaching should really begin at the time of admission. During assessment, planning and diagnosing, nurses should identify the needs and problems of the patient and his or her family, as well as their education level.
2. Document the teaching process. It is important to document your teaching from admission through discharge, as it can impact evaluation and reimbursement, as well as help newer nurses learn effective strategies. Good documentation can help maintain care continuity when the patient's care is transitioned from one nurse to the next.
3. Set goals together. From the beginning, the nurse and patient should decide together on goals and objectives, ensuring that each person understands the goals and why achieving the goals is important. Be sure to continually evaluate and reformulate goals and objectives as patient care progresses.
4. Emphasize necessary strategies. In the inpatient setting, many patients fear losing their independence. Patients will be motivated to learn what is necessary for them to care for themselves. Nurses should therefore emphasize

these strategies.

5. Timing is everything. Choose a mutually agreed upon time to teach. Look for a time that is good for both you and the patient. For example, patients that have just heard their diagnosis may need time to process that information before they are open to learning. Also, look for a time when you will not be interrupted and the patient will not be distracted by visitors, meal time, etc.

6. Know what they already know. Nurses do not want to spend time going over something that the patient already knows. That time is better spent educating or coaching the patient in other ways. If the patient already knows why they need to take a medication, but they don't always do it, perhaps the teaching time is better spent on motivating the patient to care for themselves.

7. Consider education level and literacy. Not all patients can understand complex medical terms and some may not be able to read. Other patients may be very well-educated and be familiar with medical terminology. Others may have limited English proficiency, so a medical interpreter will be needed. Tailor your teaching to each patient's level of understanding to be the most effective.

8. Seeing and hearing is believing. Customize your teaching to the patient's physical abilities. If a patient can't hear well, they may not digest verbal instructions. Those that are vision-impaired won't be able to read patient handouts.

9. Break it up. Look for those ideal teaching moments where you can impart small bits of education and engage the patient by evaluating his or her understanding. Doing this in small increments helps you and the patient. It's much easier to fit in a small teaching moment while you're in the patient's room than it is to spend a big chunk of time on discharge day. And, the patient doesn't have to digest all of the information at once.

10. Consider costs and income. Keep your recommendations practical, especially for patients on a fixed income.

www.ingramcontent.com/pod-product-compliance
Lightning Source LLC
Chambersburg PA
CBHW081145130726
47996CB00009B/2989